Denise,

Luvya Blue!

Dan Pastorini
7

TAKING
FLAK
MY LIFE IN THE FAST LANE

TAKING FLAK

MY LIFE IN THE FAST LANE

Dan Pastorini with John P. Lopez

author HOUSE®

AuthorHouse™
1663 Liberty Drive
Bloomington, IN 47403
www.authorhouse.com
Phone: 1-800-839-8640

First published by AuthorHouse   11/09/2011

ISBN: 978-1-4670-4468-4 (sc)
ISBN: 978-1-4670-4467-7 (hc)
ISBN: 978-1-4670-4466-0 (ebk)

Library of Congress Control Number: 2011917780

Printed in the United States of America

Any people depicted in stock imagery provided by Thinkstock are models, and such images are being used for illustrative purposes only.
Certain stock imagery © Thinkstock.

This book is printed on acid-free paper.

It was like Camelot. And Dante "Giuseppe" Antonio Pastorini was King. He was royalty, even to his teammates. He could throw a football 80 yards. When he walked into a room, women fell at his feet. He raced cars. He raced boats. He had a big heart. And he was one tough S.O.B. We were complete opposites, the Playboy and the Hayseed. I never knew a man like Dante Pastorini. And there never will be another like him.

■ Carl Mauck, Oilers teammate

We could not have respected Dan Pastorini more. He kept getting up. We probably hit Dan more than we hit any quarterback we played. He always showed up. He gave his team everything. When they traded Dan, things started going downhill for the Oilers.

■ "Mean" Joe Green, Steelers Hall of Famer

Jimmy Page once told me, "It's better to live one day as a lion than a thousand years as a mouse." Dan Pastorini lived everyday as a lion. He was a Renaissance man. He was James Bond. He was a rock star.

■ Mark Bowman, Photographer/Friend

Dan was a good teammate and a good guy. He played with passion. He had the toughness to continue playing despite a number of injuries, and you always knew he was going to give everything he had. He had a great arm and was a classic pocket passer. We all kidded him that he couldn't run worth a lick."

■ Ted Thompson, Green Bay Packers GM

Dan Pastorini had a larger than life personality. I was around the Oilers locker-room as a 20-year-old kid at the University of Houston, rounding up quotes. I got to know him a lot more after his playing days and really saw how much he impacted peoples' lives. He had the persona of a swashbuckling Hollywood leading man. He had that kind of swagger and was that kind of character. Dan had a special aura at a special time for football and in the City of Houston. I always thought it was appropriate that Dan became an accomplished race car driver after his playing career, because he did everything at warp speed. His story is a study in coping with stardom and celebrity in that era, and dealing with all the adversities and difficulties that go with it.

■ Jim Nantz
Voice of CBS Sports

ACKNOWLEDGEMENTS

Thank you KC Morse for her creative cover artwork & design. I would like to thank John Lopez for his friendship, undying effort and passion writing this book and leading me on a cathartic journey. Thanks to Scott Perkins for planting the seed to write this book. Thanks to my parents for their unconditional love and Pam Morse for your love and support. Thanks to Bum Phillips for guidance, friendship and love; Larry Enderli for keeping me in the race, on and off the track. Thank you to Carl Mauck, the best friend anyone could have. Thanks to Kelleyne Mackey for 40 years of friendship. God bless Mother Helen "Mother Goose" Costello. Thank you, Luv Ya Blue Oilers teammates. We were very special together! Thank you, "Luv Ya Blue" fans of the great City of Houston for undying love, respect and spirit all these years. Thanks to my friends and partners Manny Asadurian and Lee Donabedian; Rusty Weekes, Jack Zwissig, Fatty Franklin; Tick Falletti and Santa Clara University. Thanks to Thomas Coffman. Thank you, Memaw Connor, for keeping your daughter in line and filling the void of my mother. Thanks, Todd Pastorini for being the little brother I never had. Thank you, Louis "Butch" Pastorini for exemplifying courage. God bless our Troops, my family and America!

■ Dante Pastorini

ACKNOWLEDGEMENTS

I would like to thank Dante Pastorini for incredible candor, insight and hospitality in this collaboration. I would like to thank Jan for everything. I would like to thank Pam Morse for her hospitality and encouragement. I also would like to thank Jacob, BG and Leah Lopez for patience and support during this project; Jay Mincks and Insperity, Jason Cutbirth, Elizabeth Marshall of Kgbtx. communications, Meghan Allen, Suzanne Haugen, Karen Henry, John McClain, Carl Mauck, Rob Lynch, Mark Bowman, Scott Perkins, the CBS Radio family, Brahna Pastorini, Barry Warner, Kelleyne Mackey, Robbie Bohren, Michelle Schmitt, Todd Dennis, Bob Hyde, Rusty Weekes and Sam and Jo Claytor. And for being by my side literally for every word, I would like to thank Gibson.

■ John P. Lopez

For my daughter, Brahna.
Thank you, for your forgiveness and love. You are the best thing
that ever happened to me. I love you.
■ Dante Pastorini

For my beautiful wife.
■ John P. Lopez

FORWARD

By O.A. "Bum" Phillips

Dan Pastorini lived his life the way everybody ought to. He was true to his own feelings. He was just an ordinary kid with an extraordinary talent put into a difficult situation. He had money. He was good-looking. People fawned over him. Most of the time, when someone is put into that kind of situation, it's hard for them to really be themselves. But Dan always was. His true emotions showed, for better and worse. He was temperamental. When he thought something, he said it. Sometimes it got him into trouble, but I never had a problem with him.

He could throw the ball a mile and was the perfect match for Kenny Burrough. Kenny could outrun the wind, but he couldn't outrun Dan. His ability to throw the football where he wanted to throw it, and call 80—to 85-percent of the plays at the line of scrimmage, was pretty darned remarkable. There aren't many quarterbacks in the league right now that can do what Dan did. I know there won't ever be many like him. He always kept his word and took the consequences. If he went out to a bar at training camp and had a good time, if I asked him about it the next day, he'd say, "Yeah, I did it."

That's just his way. If he did it, he'd pay it. If you couldn't count on anyone else, you could count on Dan. And you couldn't keep him on the bench unless you tied him to it.

Trading Dan after the 1979 season, when we lost to Pittsburgh for the second time in the AFC Championship game, was a big mistake on my part. I should not have listened to him when he took responsibility and asked to be traded. I should not have kept my word that if a player ever asked to be traded, I would accommodate him. I should have told Dan, "You ain't going to get traded, so go on home."

But when Dan makes up his mind to do something, he does it. He commits to it and does it right. He always played that way and always lived his life that way. He stopped drinking because he just made up his mind to stop drinking. What does that tell you about the will and the heart he has? I wouldn't guess anything's going to change with this book. If he commits to telling you his story, then he's going to tell you the entire story and be honest about it all.

PROLOGUE

I was about 11-months sober when I finally saw things clearly. I sat in my car, parked on the side of Fannin Street not far from Houston's Medical Center. I stared through a chain-link fence at a vacant lot. I'm not sure what made me turn onto Fannin Street on that early-Spring day in 2011. Maybe it was an old habit. Maybe it was my mind telling me I had to go down that road again because I needed to clear my conscience. It was a fateful turn. But I have made a lot of fateful turns in my life, not all of them proud ones. I was the boy with a golden arm who never stopped trying to live up to expectations. I became one of the most scrutinized, criticized and admired quarterbacks the NFL ever knew. I raced drag boats, pushed records to the limit and was involved in a tragedy it took years to even talk about. I took on the best Top Fuel drag racers in the world and beat them. I was called a Playboy and a swashbuckler. It all flashed back to me as I sat in my car, staring at the vacant lot that was home for nine of my 13-years in the NFL. As traffic whizzed past and I stared at the overgrown lot, I thought about the wild, unpredictable ride it was. People have described my life as part-North Dallas Forty, part-Forrest Gump, part-Urban Cowboy.

This story is about that ride. I've shared parts of it in bars, bedrooms and boardrooms for more than 40-years and I guess I have done things most people only see in the movies. But just like the movies, there is so much that goes on behind the scenes.

I want it all out there. I was the rebel. I always did things fast and big. I liked speed. I liked fast cars, fast boats, fast anything. I liked fast wide receivers, fast women and fast living. Not everyone could drive a Top Fuel dragster 300-mph. But for some reason, I could. Not everyone could break speed-boat records. But I did. Not many people could get drafted by a big-league baseball team and play quarterback in the NFL. But the good Lord put a lightning bolt on my right shoulder and gave me the ability to throw a baseball over a 10-story building and a football further than any quarterback in history.

I had it all. Or, at least that's what people always said. A Playboy model and a Las Vegas showgirl were two of my eventual five wives. Women threw themselves at me. Farrah Fawcett told me she wanted to have my baby. I once was engaged to Miss Teen America. I had a fling with Vikki Lamotta and an open invitation to the Playboy Mansion. Women never were a problem. Too many women were. I hung out with Hollywood stars, made a few movies, did some TV, posed for Playgirl and drove the 24 Hours of Daytona. I was the supposed toughest man in football, suffering 12 concussions and breaking nearly 75 bones, captaining the most rebellious and untamed football squad the NFL knew.

I was the biggest reason football as we watch it and play it changed forever, throwing the ball that led to instant-replay and wearing a prototype Flak Jacket to protect three broken ribs for the remainder of the season and playoffs.

I was anti-establishment and had notorious run-ins with authority. I had a temper. I had family steal from me. I drank too much. I was addicted to pain pills. I did inhale. I did have emotional issues. I did have sex with those women. And I did say what you thought I said.

But, man, what an experience it was. It was fairy-tale. It was surreal. I was called a legend and a gunslinger. I also hit bottom more than once. Literally, face-first.

As I sat there at Fannin and Braeswood, I saw it all with clear eyes, rather than through the bottom of a bottle or the prism of ambition and gluttony. I realized I was just like that old, beautiful field. I was temporary. Weeds eventually grew around me and dirt was poured over my head. The person I always tried to be was covered up with concrete and paved over with stories of my exploits and troubles.

That's why I am writing this. It's been cathartic, but it's not just for me. It's for those who have followed me and those who will follow me. Just like in the movies, things rarely are what they seem to be. I thought I knew everything and I didn't know shit. I thought I could do anything, but I screwed up too often. I abandoned my daughter for years. I never was the husband I should have been. I got into trouble I should have avoided. I took pills and got shot up and drank too much to escape from myself. I went bankrupt, twice. I put up walls and erected an image of what I thought I should be, because in my heart I fell well short of my capabilities. I acted tough and lashed out on the outside, but I always was riddled with doubt and insecurities. Part of me always felt guilty for having things that others didn't. I always felt I had to live up to being the superstar. My successes never were enough. If I had finally beaten Pittsburgh and won a Super Bowl, it wouldn't have been enough Super Bowls. If I had won every race that I drove, I wouldn't have won enough races. If I had every tall, blonde, busty woman in America, I would have wanted more.

I've been called Barabbas and I often felt haunted the same way, like I didn't deserve the gifts I had. I've tried to forget and block out a lot of things, but I'll make no excuses. I'm going to speak from my heart. It will be painful. It will be embarrassing. It will be funny. If I'm the asshole you think I am, fine. But I'm going to tell you exactly how I got to the corner of Fannin and Braeswood in the Spring of 2011. And if I have to take some flak for it, fine. I always have.

CHAPTER ONE

"That kid's got a quarter-million dollar arm."

In the early-fall of 1948, my dad had a hunting accident. My family lived on a beautiful ten acres along Highway 49, near Yosemite Junction, at the foot of the California Sierra Nevada Mountains. Dante Pastorini Sr. sank his life savings into those ten acres, chasing the American dream. On those rare days when dad could get away from working as a butcher, school bus driver, part-time carpenter and one hustling, horse-trading S.O.B., it was hunting that was his passion. Deer hunting, hog hunting, bird hunting. Dad and mom, Dorothy, earned every dollar they made. They busted their asses, bought everything they could with cash, lived modestly and saved the rest. When they finally saved enough to buy a piece of land where they could raise their family near Sonora, Calif., my dad and grandfather, Lou, who immigrated from Tuscany, built a house along a creek at the back of a 10-acre parcel at the foot of the Sierra Nevadas. They built the house by hand, clearing trees, dragging away shale and river rocks, cutting and framing the lumber and running plumbing and electricity lines.

Dad's love for the outdoors probably was the biggest reason he chose to settle his family along that tucked-away piece of Tuolumne County that once was the heart of the California Gold Rush. By 1948 the Gold Rush had long been dead and

Highway 49 was well off the beaten path, but dad still had big dreams. He wanted to build and open a restaurant along the front of the property near the highway. A lot of Italian-Americans settled in Tuolumne County after the Gold Rush, which lured my grandfather's family. My Grandmother Irma's family also was from the old country, emigrating from Genoa. Just about every family in Tuolumne County had some kind of roots to the Gold Rush. About $600 million worth of gold eventually was mined from the area between the Sierra Nevadas, Sonora Pass and Tioga Pass. And right in the middle of it all were those ten acres. The Sierra Nevadas literally were at the back door and old, abandoned gold mines, railroad tracks and passes cut in and out of the landscape all around. It was called Yosemite Junction for a reason. It was the pass tourists took to get to Yosemite National Park.

Mom and dad figured tourists and local families needed a good restaurant, where they could stop, get a good meal and enjoy the amazing views. The land was lush, with plenty of wildlife, creeks, brush and all kinds of different trees–oak, pine, maple, dogwood. Sonora may not have been what it once was, but tourists kept it alive. One thing about my dad, he always was thinking. He always had a plan. Mom's biggest hope was the restaurant would keep the family together and living in the country would be perfect for the family to spend a lot of time together. Dorothy, the oldest, was twelve in 1948 and was named after my mother. Annette was seven. And then there was Lou, who everybody called Butch, and was five. It wasn't until my dad finished his hunting trip that day in 1948 that I came into the picture. When dad got home, he realized he spent most of the afternoon sitting in poison oak. He was covered in oil residue from the Poison Oak. It would be just a matter of hours until most of his body would be covered with a rash and he'd be quite uncomfortable for a long time. Those were the days when Poison Oak could last two weeks or maybe even a month or more. It was treated mostly with home remedies–things like oatmeal and baking soda. So my dad brainstormed, as always, and decided to make the most of the situation. He decided he should get amorous with mom before he broke out in the rash, because it might be a while before he could again.

Surprise. Nine months later, I was born Dante Anthony Pastorini Jr. I was the hunting accident, the youngest of four, and five years younger than my nearest sibling. Barely six months after I was born, with an extra mouth to feed that they did not expect or plan, my parents opened Pastorini's Longhorn Club and Café. They came up with the name because dad was kind of a cowboy. He loved horses, always had horses and of course, loved the outdoors. Dad, along with my grandfather and some friends built the restaurant at the front of our property. It was wood-framed, with hardwood floors and great scenery all-around. There was a big dining room, with a bar in front and a club and banquet room in back. Dad was the butcher, wheeler-dealer and cook. Mom was hostess, ran the kitchen and did some cooking. The kids pitched in busing tables, cleaning the restaurant and helping in the kitchen. I learned to walk in that restaurant and did a little bit of everything as I grew up. I learned to hustle for everything just like my dad, who took pride in being meticulous about everything he did. His knives were like treasures. He sharpened them to the point they sliced through loins of beef like butter. Dad cut a loin of beef so closely there wouldn't be enough meat left on the bone for a dog. He was a master butcher. And none of us could ever touch his knives. Ever. He was crazy obsessive about them. He'd yell at us, telling us we were going to dull the edges. Dad had all the connections for restaurant supplies and equipment, too. He drove into town in his truck, with a tarp over the bed. He came back with crates of produce, supplies for the restaurant and sides of beef that he would cut himself. He traded crates of this for crates of that. He was a horse-trading son of a gun. He also always found a way to get people into the restaurant. He was proud of his food and it was always good, but he always was thinking of ways to make the place a destination. There were some lean times, especially early when the club at the back of the restaurant was closed just three months after the restaurant opened. The Feds came in and shut it down, because all clubs were getting licensed and were under scrutiny because of changing gambling laws.

Even though some times were tougher than others, we never lacked. We did learn the value of a dollar, certainly. When dad realized neither the seasonal tourism nor just 1,300 people living in Sonora was enough to sustain the restaurant, he cleared a piece of our property and put in a small rodeo arena. It fit in perfectly with the cowboy theme of the restaurant. He bulldozed an oval, cleared the land and put up a fence. We always had horses anyway, so dad began having rodeos on Saturdays and Sundays. By the time I was six, Butch and I would spend Saturdays sitting on the fence, roping calves after events, corralling animals and getting people to stop by the restaurant for a steak, some home-style meals or Italian food.

I always looked up to Butch. I thought he was the best athlete in the world, too. We probably were the closest among the kids. Mom had a constant dream of us becoming a certain type of family. She always wanted us to do everything together and be a close family that loved each other unconditionally. But we never were what she dreamed about. We all went to church, worked together and mom made sure we were good Catholics, but we really all started going our own ways at an early age. No one ever really showed a lot of affection in our house, except for mom. Dad never told any of us that he loved us and dad's big shortcoming was his temper. When something didn't go right at the restaurant or there'd be some other problem, he'd scream at my mom or throw something. There was a lot of pressure on him with four kids and the life-changing decision he made to open a business in a town of 1,300 people. He also went way over the top sometimes. Mom took a lot of crap from all of us, in fact. Dorothy and Annette never really got along, always seemed to be jealous of each other and were entirely different types of people. Dorothy was the wild child, going out, smoking, drinking, carousing. Annette was kind of a strange cat. She was just a different personality, kind of plain, with a good old-fashioned Italian nose and a quiet side. My dad teased Annette a lot.

"If I could fill that nose with nickels, I'd be a rich man," he'd tell her.

I guess that's the only way our family knew how to show affection. We teased each other until we cut to the bone.

Butch was short and muscular and the toughest kid around, with a temper like my dad. When I was seven, Butch and I got into a snow ball fight with some kids who were Butch's age. One of the kids put a rock inside a snowball and hit me over the eye with it, cutting my eye pretty good. Butch just exploded. I mean, it was a 20-minute ass-kicking. When the kid got knocked down,

Butch picked him back up and beat him some more. All the way down the highway, Butch was beating his ass. I got scared and ran back to the restaurant to tell dad Butch was fighting. As he watched from the porch, dad took a puff of his cigarette and said, "Let him fight."

Then, dad yelled at the kid running up the highway, "Don't ever come back you little son of a bitch, because I'll do it next time."

A few months later, we were clearing another area on the property for a barn. Butch and I were out messing around when Butch went behind a huge oak to cut a willow switch with his pocket knife. A friend of dad's was working a bulldozer, cutting down the oak tree. He never saw Butch standing behind the tree.

When the driver hollered at us to clear the area, my dad thought Butch was with us. Dad grabbed me and said, "Come on, Willie."

Dad always called me Willie because from the moment I saw Willie Mays a couple years earlier in the 1954 World Series, he was my hero. He was my idol. The Say-Hey Kid seemed perfect to me.

When dad and I turned around, Butch wasn't with us. Just as we heard the crack of the tree falling, we saw him behind the tree. It had an L-shaped branch pointing out the back, toward where Butch was standing. Butch ran away when he heard the crack of the tree, but he slipped on some sharp shale rock. The tree hit him and the limb dragged him across the rock. Dad and I ran toward Butch, screaming, "Are you alright? Are you alright?"

"Yeah, I think so."

But when Butch stood up and tried to take a step, the entire quad muscle on his right leg squeezed out the front of his thigh. The shale cut a wide gash up the front of Butch's leg, from the top of his knee, to his hip joint. When he stood up, the skin just laid wide open, like someone sliced open a banana. The gash was so deep; dad and I could see the bone.

Butch was 13-years-old, but he never shed a tear. Right there, I gained so much admiration for Butch and I realized just how tough he was. Eventually, Butch underwent several operations, skin grafts, had his leg set and re-set and had several hundred stitches. The scar was horrible. Naturally, I made fun of it. The next year, Butch wanted to play football and he made the middle school football team basically on one leg. That's the kid I decided I wanted to be like. Dad always bragged about Butch's successes in sports, too. Butch truly set the tone for me. I'd better not cry about anything. I'd better be tough. I'd better be good. Watching my dad admire Butch so much, I always wanted that admiration. I wanted that affirmation from dad.

Even before I started playing organized baseball, I played thousands of imaginary games on our property. We had a creek behind our house and there was every kind of rock imaginable in that creek bed. I was Willie Mays. I pretended I was making the throw from center-field in the 1954 World Series, throwing rocks all the way down the gravel road that ran from the house at the back, to the highway. I pretended to catch a ball over my shoulder, then turned and chunked rocks as far as I could. I did it over and over again. I wrapped tape around old broomsticks from the restaurant and hit rocks from the gravel road over the creek or from the back of the restaurant across the property. I was Willie

Mays, bottom of the ninth, throwing rocks up and hitting them. I hunted with rocks, too. I hiked up the Sierra Nevadas with a BB gun and climbed through old mining dumps and up and down rocks and cliffs, shooting mice, or throwing rocks at mice and birds. Butch and I made up a bunch of competitions, too. He was older and better than me at most games, but it didn't take long before I started wearing his ass out. It was about 60-yards from the front of the restaurant to the back and we would see which one of us could throw a rock all the way to the back. By the time I was eight, I was throwing better than Butch, easily throwing a rock over the restaurant. I also started playing organized baseball and it just came easy. I never knew why, but throwing a ball just felt natural, and simple. It also was weird that I couldn't throw with my left hand. I did my homework left-handed, ate left-handed, washed dishes and bused tables left-handed. I did most everything left-handed. But when I picked up a rock, a baseball or a football, I would rear back with my right arm, reach far back behind until my arm was parallel to the ground and sling it overhead with ease. I was a pitcher and shortstop. My first year playing organized baseball, I threw eight no-hitters. My second year, I threw nine. I struck out batter after batter after batter. When I pitched well, dad bragged about me and that's the closest he ever got to telling me he loved me. I craved the attention. When I was in third-grade, I played left-field on my brother's eighth-grade team. Sometimes, I tried to figure out why it was me that was given this gift. As much as I was having fun playing with the older kids, earning a lot of attention, especially from my dad, I felt a little bit of a burden and a responsibility. My dad always told Butch, mom, and just about everyone, "That kid's got a quarter-million dollar arm."

I always wanted to please dad, play well for my coaches and live up to everything that Butch was as a player. The more I pitched in Little League, the harder I threw. The more success I had, the more I threw. It always was to please dad. My dream was to look him in the eye one day and say, "We did it."

Dad never got his chance to make it, even though he was a hell of a baseball player. As a teenager in the 1930s, dad was a catcher for the San Francisco Mission Reds of the Pacific Coast League. He played with guys like Joe DiMaggio and Lefty O'Doul. He loved all kinds of sports, but baseball was No. 1. He was a special player. When he was eighteen, playing at the Double-A level for the Mission Reds, a New York Yankees scout discovered him. After scouting my dad, the scout went to my grandparents' house and talked about bringing dad to New York, putting him in the organization and making a big-league player out of him. He offered my dad a baseball contract, but my grandmother refused to allow dad to sign.

"My son is not going to be a bum," she told dad. "My son is going to get an honest job and make an honest living."

Dad begged his parents to let him play for the Yankees, but they refused. They thought ballplayers were low-class people. They thought ballplayers were uneducated. It always ate at dad that he didn't get his chance. So I wanted to fulfill that dream for him.

To me, my grandparents were crotchety and kind of mean. I knew they did a lot of good things and were good people, but I never really got to know them, because they spoke only Italian. They were first-generation Pastorinis from the Old Country. My sister Dorothy was bilingual, but by the time I was eight, she already was long gone to college. Being the youngest, I never learned anything but a couple of words in Italian. My mother was Irish and she wound up speaking better Italian than dad, but I never talked with my grandparents. All I knew was they were old; they were real tough on dad and never really wanted to spend a lot of time with us kids.

My grandfather died when I was nine. I was outside playing by myself near the creek. I was throwing rocks behind a huge walnut tree, when I heard someone come outside the back of the restaurant. It was dad and he was crying. I ducked behind the tree. I was just scared, because I'd never seen my father cry before. This was my hero. This was the strongest man I knew. And he just kept crying. I finally walked up to him and put my arm around him. He kept weeping. I asked what was wrong and he told me his father died.

It hit him right there that he wished he would have told his father that he loved him. Or maybe he wished his father would have told him. Dad felt a tremendous loss. Seeing dad like that weighed heavily on me for a long time. I never before saw that kind of pain and anguish on his face.

CHAPTER TWO

Catholic Guilt

I often saw a kind of distant look on mom's face. It bothered me. She wanted our family to be that perfect picture she had in her head when they bought the property outside Sonora. It killed her that her kids were selfish little asses. She was a great lady that did so much for us, but it always bothered her that my sisters never could get along and mom was out of the loop with the one interest that dad, Butch and I always shared–sports. She mentioned once at the breakfast table when Butch and I were talking about the San Francisco Giants.

"Sports, sports, sports. Why can't you ever talk about anything else?"

Butch told her, "Well, mom, what do you want to talk about? We'll talk about whatever you want, mom."

She just welled up in tears, slammed the pan she had in her hand into the sink and walked away.

It was a losing battle she fought. By the time my grandfather died, Dorothy already was off to college, Annette was in high school and kind of distant, Butch was going into Sonora High School. I spent a lot of time alone, playing imaginary games. I had a lot of imaginary friends. I played Army. I hiked. I hunted. I'd throw rocks, over and over, at targets all over our land. I'd try to throw rocks over bridges. I tried to knock twigs off of trees. I tried to hit knots on trees. It was a strange life, really.

I probably was happiest alone when I was racing my quarter-midget race car. Sitting in that car was comforting. I learned to drive when I was seven, driving my dad's '49 Coupe up and down the gravel road on our land. It had a column-shift, so I literally hung from the steering wheel while I pressed the clutch and shifted. The roar of the engine fascinated me. Race cars fascinated me. I collected racing magazines and spent a lot of time with Jim Opie, who owned Opie's Garage in Columbia. He had quarter-midget go-carts at his place and I'd watch him work on engines and marvel at those cars. I pestered my parents enough that I finally got my own quarter-midget car and I treated it like it was an Indy 500 racer. I polished it two or three times a day. My dad saw how much I drove that thing, how much I loved it and asked me how many kids I thought had cars. I told him there were quarter-midget races all over California. That's when he decided to turn the rodeo arena into a 10th-of-a-mile oval dirt track. It was the only quarter-midget track in the county. Anything that would bring people into the restaurant, my dad did it. The track really turned out to be pretty good for business. We would put on races every Friday and Saturday. We would get kids that raced to come with their families and sometimes people would show up just to watch. They usually would eat at our restaurant. People would sit in the restaurant bar, too, watching us race. I loved it. I felt like I had an audience and I always won my share of races. I kept the track groomed and watered and organized races. At baseball games, school events, in Sonora and Columbia, at church, I talked to kids about racing. Sometimes we raced at dusk and dads would park their cars around the track so we could race under the lights. Sometimes, kids from other towns like Oakdale and Jamestown would come in to race against us.

That little track, along with the University of Pacific refurbishing the old Fallon House Theater in Columbia saved mom and dad's business. The Fallon House was an old theater built during the Gold Rush days. The University restored it for Summer Stock shows. It brought more tourists and a lot of actors. About the same time, NBC was filming the TV series Tales Of Wells Fargo on the outskirts of Sonora and Columbia, which wasn't too far away. It brought more folks into the Longhorn Club & Café. All of the stars in the series, especially Ralph Bellamy and Dale Robertson, loved my dad's food.

By the time I was 12, I was the only kid left at home. Annette went to San Jose State, then went on to work for the State Department. Dorothy went to college and married young, to a law student named Stan House and Butch went to Santa Clara to play football. Butch was a hell of a player, even though he was only 5-foot-9 and about 200-pounds. Butch knocked the piss out of everyone he hit on a football field. He was real good. When he brought it, he brought it all. He had no fear. He'd take on anyone.

I spent most of my time playing baseball or flag-football at Sonora Grammar School, racing my car, hiking, hunting or working in the restaurant. I got my spending money sweeping up nickels and dimes that customers and dad dropped on the floor. That's how he got us to work so hard and fast—he'd grab a handful of change and toss it on the floor after the restaurant closed. As we swept, we picked up change. I bused tables and earned a few tips, after I learned what a tip was. A customer flagged me down one day and tried to give me a dollar. I told him I couldn't take his money. He was trying to give me a tip, but mom and dad always told me not to take anything from strangers. Mom saw what was happening and told me, "Son, this is alright. It's for your good work. This is a tip."

She smiled and then did something weird. She asked me to sign the dollar bill. She said she would always keep that dollar bill in a safe place for me, so I could always remember my first dollar and no matter what, I always would have enough money to call home. I signed it and she put it away. I wound up always having a little money in my pocket working at the restaurant–at least enough to get by.

I already was dreaming of bigger things; of someday going pro in baseball or football. One dollar never would be that important to me. I made every All Star team in baseball and I was the best quarterback in flag-football. When I watched the Packers on TV, I dreamed of playing in the NFL. When I watched baseball, I dreamed of being in the big-leagues. When I watched racing, I dreamed of driving in the Indy 500. By the time I got to high school, one thing I knew for sure was I wanted to get out of Sonora. I loved the place and it was home, but I never wanted to be just another guy from Sonora. Half the guys in town usually wound up getting a girl knocked up and never left the place. They'd work for a lumber company or energy company and never experience anything outside the county. That's not what I wanted. Those might have been great lives and they might have had great families, but I had a different ambition.

I knew I was a talented athlete. I always was pretty bashful and did a lot of things alone, but I was a popular kid in school because I could play sports. Sports opened a lot of doors for me socially. Had it not been for what I could do on the field, I probably wouldn't have had many friends. I had big dreams and finally talked to mom and dad about going away to Bellarmine College Preparatory for high school. Mom and dad always told Butch he could go to a place where there might be better opportunities in academics and sports. Butch had a chance to go to Bellarmine, which was a real good school and a football powerhouse coached by John Hanna. There were great coaches like Bill McPherson and Bob Mazzucca at Bellarmine and their teams always had all-state and all-American players. Guys who went to Bellarmine got noticed and earned scholarships. That's what I wanted. When Butch was headed to high school, he took the Bellarmine entrance exam, passed it and was admitted. But at the last moment he backed out. He didn't want to live 130-miles away in San Jose. I didn't care. In fact, I wanted to get out. I was at home alone all the time, anyway. Besides, I wanted to out-do Butch. I wanted to do something he didn't do. I passed the exam and enrolled. The first night I was at Bellarmine, I already was homesick. Standing in chow line, I was thinking I made a huge mistake. Then, some kid in front of me in a blue windbreaker turns around, sticks out his hand and says, "I'm Rusty Weekes."

Rusty and I became roommates and fast friends. Rusty helped me realize I was in the right spot. Bellarmine had one of the most competitive environments anywhere. I loved it. It wasn't just sports. The debate team had to be the best. The school newspaper had to win awards. Everything had to be the best.

When I got to football tryouts, I lined up with the linebackers and running backs. I never played either position before. The coaches didn't know I played quarterback in grammar school. Since Ray Nitschke was my hero, I tried out for linebacker. Since I always pretended I was Jim Taylor, I thought I could play running back. I couldn't do either. I was trying out against guys who came from city leagues and had played contact football for years. After a week of tryouts, Coach John Lounibos, the freshman coach, came up to me and said, "I'm sorry. This sport may not be for you. You're not ready to play at this level. I'm going to have to cut you."

That's when the Pastorini temper came out. I couldn't believe I was getting cut. I never got cut from anything. I turned my back on coach, picked up a football, and fired the ball as hard as I could across the field, screaming, just completely pissed off. The football went about 65-yards.

"Come here, son," coach told me. "You ever play quarterback before?"

"Yeah, that's all I've ever played. I thought I'd try something else."

I made the team with that one throw. And we were dominant. My freshman, sophomore and junior seasons, the Bellarmine Bels went 36-1. My junior year, we platooned three full offenses. We broke teams down physically. We set a record that can never be broken. We went undefeated and our defense was un-scored upon. The only points any opponent scored on us came on a batted ball returned for a touchdown. It didn't take long for me to gain a lot of recognition as a strong-armed quarterback. I was one of California's elite blue-chippers. I earned all-star accolades, played in the East-West High School Shrine Game and I could easily throw the ball 75-yards.

As the awards and accolades kept piling up, I was worried some of the attention I was getting as a big-time college prospect may have bothered Butch. He was a great player at Santa Clara, earning Little All-America honors on offense and defense. He was just too small to play at a bigger school and when his college career ended, he wasn't going to get a chance as a pro. On Memorial Day, I took a girlfriend skiing with Butch, his wife and their new son, Todd. A fuel clamp broke on the boat. I went into town to get one, but it took me four hours, because all the garages and parts stores were closed for the holiday. Butch thought I was out messing around or I blew off trying to get the clamp. When I finally came back with the clamp, he was pissed off and hot from sitting out in the sun. His wife was hot; the baby was hot and crying. Butch walked up to me and punched me square in the jaw, knocking me on my ass. I got so mad and was hurt at the same time. I challenged him to meet me at the house for an ass-kicking. I was fuming. It was a turning point in our relationship. He had always been hard on me, but he'd never done something like this. When he got to the house, I was raging, but he just walked up to me, hugged me and said he was sorry. Butch always was the big star in the family. Subconsciously, it was hard for him to cope with me reaching another level. It ate at him that I was coming on strong. I told him, "If it wasn't for you, Butch, I never would have achieved anything."

My senior year, I had a good year, but we lost three games and it felt like a losing season to us. One of the teams we lost to was Pittsburgh. Go figure. By the end of the season, I was being recruited by a lot of different colleges–several Ivy League schools, Cal, Stanford, UCLA, USC. Stanford was interesting and I liked Dick Vermeil, who was recruiting me, but they had just signed Jim Plunkett, who went to James Lick High School not far from Bellarmine. From the time I was a freshman, all I ever heard about was Jim Plunkett, who was a grade above me. I'm sure he got tired of hearing about me, too. Everybody compared him to me and me to him.

I almost signed with UCLA, but I couldn't deal with Tommy Prothro's bullshit and couldn't help but call him out on it. When I met with coach Prothro on a visit to UCLA, he wrote seven names on a chalkboard and started telling me all the reasons I should sign with the Bruins. I knew most of the names. They were the best quarterbacks in California. My name was at the bottom of the list and Prothro started going down names, pointing at each with a piece of chalk and saying some things about each player.

"These are the quarterbacks UCLA is recruiting. This guy is a real talented passer, but his arm isn't quite what I'm looking for. This guy is the fastest quarterback and a real good leader. This guy has a chance to be a pretty good quarterback . . ."

He went down the list. Then he got to my name. He slammed the piece of chalk onto the board, circled my name and said, "But THIS GUY. This guy right here! He's going to be the next great one. He's going to be the guy who replaces Gary Beban."

I kind of nodded my head, then said to Prothro, "That sounds great, coach. But have you told those other six guys that I'm going to be starting?"

He just looked at me like, "You smart ass."

Yeah, I was. I got my temper from my dad, my smart-ass habit of always saying what I thought from my brother and my poise from my mom. Some people questioned why I signed with Santa Clara, when I could have gone anywhere. I was just confident in myself that I could go to the same school my brother did, the same school my best friend Rusty Weekes was going to attend, and still reach my dreams. It also was because of Coach Pat Malley. He was a great man and a good coach. When he recruited me, he said, "I'm only going to guarantee you one thing and it has nothing to do with football. If you come here, you're going to have a free ride to the best education of your life. If you're good enough, you're going to play pro. They'll find you here. If you're good enough, the pros always find you."

Rusty was headed to Santa Clara to play baseball and would be my roommate again. After I committed to the Broncos, I was drafted by the New York Mets. I thought a long time about signing with the Mets, even though they took me in the 32nd round because they knew I wanted to play football and baseball in college. I thought about the opportunity my dad lost with the Yankees. I decided the best thing to do would be to give myself more time to sort out whether I wanted to play football or baseball, so I stayed with the Broncos.

I played on the freshmen baseball team and backed up Ray Calcagno and Bobby Rickard on the varsity football teams. After that first year, I earned an invitation to play for the Alaska Goldpanners, one of the best summer amateur baseball teams in the world. They were scheduled to play on a Goodwill Tour through Japan in the summer. I had heard of a lot of the guys that were invited to be on the team. Dave Kingman, Bob Boone,

Brent Strom. I still thought maybe baseball would be my best chance to make a living doing something I loved.

Truthfully, if I thought I could have made a profitable career out of it, I probably would have chosen auto racing out of the three sports. Even as I was playing football and baseball, I always raced. Every chance I could, I would head to Freemont Raceway and enter my car in some kind of match race. I'd pay a dollar and race some guy, then do it again. When I graduated from Bellarmine, my parents bought me a 1967 Chevelle SS 396. It was all horsepower. I raced the hell out of that car. Before every race, just as I did before every game I played, I said a little prayer that Mother Cassell–we called her, "Mother Goose"—taught me at Bellarmine when I was a sophomore.

"Lord, help me to do with you, what I can't do without you."

It was just my little reminder to race or play totally free of nervousness, because somebody had more control than I did, anyway. I never worried about getting injured. I never worried about making a bad play or doing anything but going full-blast on every play or in every race. That little prayer helped me earn the reputation of a free-spirited player in high school and got me off to a good start at Santa Clara. People said I was unafraid. Sportswriters described me as tough and gutsy. Maybe believing in that prayer did make me that kind of guy, because off the field I was extremely conservative. At Bellarmine, I served Mass and never got into a lot of wild stuff. As a freshman at Santa Clara, I was low-key. It was the era of long hair and sandals, but I wore a flat-top and loafers. The hippie movement was all over TV, in magazines and on college campuses, especially in California, but

I was the clean-cut all-American boy. There was Viet Nam, all kinds of political sit-ins and demonstrations, but none of that interested me. My only vice was girls. I always had a girlfriend–at least one. Toward the end of my first year at Santa Clara, I got a girl pregnant. Part of me wanted to call the Mets and see if I still could play and just start making a living. Both of us knew her pregnancy would devastate our Catholic families. We talked about getting married. Her parents and my parents were devastated. It was a Scarlet Letter thing. It was Catholic guilt. We had this shame come into our lives, a stain on our family names. It was embarrassing and I didn't live up to what was expected of me. I just saw the pain on my parents' faces. We decided to put up the baby for adoption.

That's when I took the offer to go to Alaska and play for the Goldpanners. I just wanted to get away. It all got swept under the rug. It was the ostrich thing—just bury your head in the sand. That's how my family handled a lot of problems, we refused to face them. I got a call that the baby was born and was adopted.

I never saw the baby. All I knew was it was a boy.

CHAPTER THREE

"You'll have the world by the tail."

It was difficult dealing with the emotions of giving up a son I never got to see. I dealt with it on baseball diamonds in Fairbanks, Alaska and 5,000-miles away in Japan. Whenever I stepped onto a field or behind the wheel of a car, nothing in my personal life ever lingered. Those were my safe places. That's just the way it always was with me. Between the white lines or in a cockpit, I found sanctuary and relief. That's what happened when I joined the Alaska Goldpanners. It was a team of hitters and unbelievable talent and I fit right in. I mean, I tore the cover off the ball from the day I got there. Altogether, I batted over .350, hit with power. I drove in runs, stole bases and made some real good plays, after moving to right-field because of my arm strength. It was great for me to play with guys who were every bit as talented as me. When we took a seventeen-day, seven-city tour of Japan to face several Japanese all-star teams, my troubles literally were thousands of miles away. We played in front of the Emperor. We learned a lot about the Japanese culture and were treated like kings. When we landed, Japanese people were hanging over the rails at the airport, trying to get a look at us. There were bands, cheerleaders, women in Kimono dresses and a lot of pageantry at every stadium. We played pretty well, too. Brent Strom and Jim Barr were our best pitchers, Bob Boone was fantastic and Dave Kingman was the wildcard that hit towering home runs. He scared the hell out of me when he pitched. He was the wildest pitcher I ever saw. He threw almost 100-mph, but couldn't hit a target to save his life. The first time I hit against him in batting practice, Kingman threw a fastball behind my head. I froze up. I walked out of the box, put down my bat and told our coach, Red Boucher, "I'm not hitting against him again."

And I never did. Kingman did hit the longest homerun I ever saw at Growden Park in Fairbanks. It went at least 500-feet. I hit what would have been about a 400-foot homerun at Growden Park earlier, but the ball hit some power lines and bounced back into play. Kingman's shot went over the same power lines and looked like it still was going up. Playing for the Goldpanners, taking the trip to Japan and playing alongside great players made me feel like a big-time player and helped me move on from the situation back home.

At Santa Clara, I had a class with Sandy Roberts, who won the Miss Teenage America pageant the year before. One of the girls she beat in the competition was Cybill Shepherd, who won Miss Congeniality. Miss America and the blue-chip quarterback were in the same class. Santa Clara wasn't a very big place, so everyone on campus was wondering when Sandy and I would date. One day in class, Sandy tapped me on the shoulder and handed me a piece of paper with her phone number. We got pretty serious pretty quickly. Sandy was a beautiful girl and she definitely knew how to go after exactly what she wanted. I wished my football career got off to as fast a start. On the first snap of the first game of my sophomore season against Cal-Poly, I fumbled the snap and broke my ankle. A defensive lineman rolled into me trying to fall on the fumble. I was being touted as the next great player, but entering my junior year I still didn't have a lot of time on the field. All people knew about me was I supposedly had a golden arm. All they knew were stories about how far I could throw a baseball and a football. The story that became legend happened when I was hanging out with some baseball friends on a plaza outside Swig Hall on campus. Someone dared me to try and throw a baseball over Swig Hall, which was a 10-story dorm. I didn't really think I could do it, but, what can I say, I took the challenge. I grabbed a baseball, reared back and slung the first one as hard as I could. It hit the roof, but didn't go over. I grabbed another baseball, took a couple of steps and launched it. It sailed over everything and into the street on the other side. It became a legendary thing on campus. For the next year, people tried to match my feat. I never heard of anyone who did. A lot of times walking across campus or in a class, classmates asked me, "Did you really throw a baseball over Swig Hall?"

"Yeah, I did. But the catcher missed the tag."

My luck never got any better on the field. I got off to a great start to the season my junior year. I was clicking. We went 3-0, I was slinging it all over and we outscored our opponents 114-32. But in the fourth game against Villanova, I tore the Medial Collateral ligament in my left knee and was done for the year. It was such a frustrating thing. I could play with pain and had spurts of putting it all together, but my seasons kept getting derailed. I was just getting hit wrong.

I got to know our trainer Henry Schmidt better than anyone else on the team. Schmitty was an institution. He could chew on a cigar, tell a big story and wrap an ankle perfectly without even looking down at your foot. Schmitty saw hundreds of great NFL players come through the East-West Shrine Game, where he had been the trainer for more than 20-years. He also was the trainer for the San Francisco 49ers and Los Angeles Rams. On a wall on one side of his training room, there were pictures of all sorts of All-Americans and NFL stars that he knew.

"Schmitty, you gonna put my picture up on that wall someday?" I asked him.

"Oh, yeah. You can write your own ticket, kid. You'll have the world by the tail. I know you will. I know these things. You're gonna have the world by the tail someday."

My senior year I lasted just two games before I tore the MCL again. All my plans went to shit. That was it, I believed. Two knee injuries in two years. Who's going to draft me now? When I saw dad after getting hurt–once again, against Villanova—I just broke down and cried like a baby. I thought my dream of playing pro football was over. A few days later after talking with Schmitty, I realized I still could get back on the field for the last couple of games. I decided no way I was going to end my college career hurt, no matter what happened with the NFL. I rehabbed and ran on it for a month. I wrapped my knee, went to see Schmitty every day, and I got back in time for the last two games. We won both games and I played well. My only shot at impressing NFL scouts now was to play in as many All Star games as I could. I earned an invitation to the East-West Shrine Game at Oakland Coliseum, just up the road.

And I was hoping to match up somewhere along the line with Plunkett. Ever since my freshman year in high school, I was compared to him and he was compared to me. I wanted to show all the scouts I could play against big-time college talent. While I kept getting injured, Plunkett won the Heisman Trophy, but that didn't matter to me. I never got my chance to face off against him. When I went to the Shrine Game, he went to the Hula Bowl. When I went to the Senior Bowl, he happened to skip that game.

The Shrine Game put me on everybody's radar again. I played quarterback, I punted, I kicked. I became the only son of a Shriner to play in the Shrine game and the competition level was better than any other game. We had guys like Dan Dierdorf and Mel Gray. The Shrine Game was considered the epitome of college All Star games. The scouts wanted me to play against big-time talent, so I took the attitude, I don't care who I play against. I could play with anybody on any level. Playing quarterback always was a chess game to me. I put my strength against your weakness and I took advantage of it. I was calling plays since I was a freshman in high school. I watched Johnny Unitas, I watched Roman Gabriel, Bart Starr, Joe Kapp. That's how I learned the game. Those were my idols.

Before I got to the Shrine Game in early-January of 1971, I started running everyday on campus. I did a lot of running, a lot of drills and a lot of throwing and punting. I did isometrics, worked on my technique and begged guys to stay out with me, so I could throw to them. That's how I worked. When I got to the Shrine Game practices, I took every snap as if I was playing for my life, and I was. There were three quarterbacks on the West roster and we alternated equally–Chuck Hixson of SMU, Dennis Dummit of UCLA and me. I wasn't about to let those guys out-play me.

Against these–quote, unquote–big-time college players, I finally was side-by-side with big-school quarterbacks. I wound up being voted team captain. Before the game, I said Mother Goose's prayer, as always.

"Lord, help me to do with you what I can't do without you."

I played a great game and won the Most Valuable Player award. I threw the game-winning 45-yard touchdown pass to Mel Gray, who beat the defensive back from Northwestern, Rick Telander. I also kicked a 42-yard field-goal and punted. My performance got me into the Senior Bowl. Again, I went in hoping to go toe-to-toe with every other quarterback and taking every snap that I could. I was voted team captain along with Jack Youngblood. Lynn Dickey, J.D. Hill, John Riggins and Isiah Robertson also played. Jack wound up winning Most Valuable Defensive Player and I won Most Valuable Offensive Player. I punted, kicked four extra-points, kicked a field goal and threw a touchdown pass.

More and more scouts were going out on a limb, calling me the best quarterback in the draft. The knee injuries still had some doubting me, but in all the one-on-one conversations I had, nothing gave me more hope than listening to Bobby Beathard from the San Diego Chargers and King Hill from the Houston Oilers.

Beathard told me, "I'd really like to draft you, Dan. But I don't think you're going to be around at No. 13."

When I heard that, I thought, "Man, I guess I will get my shot."

Then I read some articles about 1971 being the, "Year of the Quarterback."

Never before were three quarterbacks chosen among the top 10 picks in the NFL Draft. But sportswriters talked about Plunkett, Archie Manning and me all going in the top ten. I couldn't believe it. Plunkett was the coverboy Heisman winner. Manning was a cult hero from the Deep South. And then there was me. I was called the California boy, a gunslinger.

The night before the draft, I was back at Santa Clara, partying with all my friends at our off-campus dorm, which was an old Travel Lodge converted into a dorm. We stumbled across the street to the Bronco Bar, then drank some more back in my room until about three in the morning. Sandy broke up with me during the season, so I spent most of my senior year enjoying college life. At one point I was dating three girls at the same time, juggling that and football. By the end of the season, each of the three girls was suspicious and heard about the other girls I was seeing. I didn't know if it was planned or how it happened, but after our last game, all three of them showed up outside the locker-room. They stood there, side-by-side-by-side. One of my teammates told me, "You've got a situation outside." I don't know if they wanted me to pick one girl or they all three were going to confront me. I called an audible and ducked out the back door.

I never figured out what it was, exactly, that I wanted out of a relationship, other than the obvious. Beyond the physical thing, I always felt I had to get married. Maybe it was because mom always wanted that perfect family and I wanted to fulfill that dream for her. I met a girl named Pat Heath at a bar in Santa Clara not long after the Shrine Game and we started dating pretty seriously. I didn't know what the hell I was doing. I just kept looking for something. I had this picture of what I was supposed to be and what I was supposed to do and it wasn't anything like what I wanted. Pat was with us the night before the draft. Rusty Weekes and all the guys I ran with at Santa Clara were there, too. There really wasn't any way to hear about the draft and we didn't have a TV in the dorm. A little after eight in the morning, a few reporters showed up to take pictures and do some interviews. There were beer bottles and beer cans all over the dorm. I cleared all the empty bottles and cans from one side of the room and stood there in front of the reporters, answering questions and taking pictures. All my buddies were on the opposite side of the room, surrounded by bottles and cans on tables, chairs, shelves, and making faces at me from behind the reporters' backs, trying to get me to laugh.

It didn't take long before the phone rang and I heard a voice say, "Dan Pastorini?"

"Yes, this is me."

"This is Ed Hughes of the Houston Oilers. We just drafted you in the first-round."

I was overwhelmed. I thought, "Thank you, Jesus."

The weight of the world was lifted off my shoulders. Just a couple months earlier I was crying in my father's arms, thinking I was done. The Boston Patriots took Plunkett No. 1, the New Orleans Saints took Archie Manning No. 2 and I went No. 3. It was the first time three quarterbacks topped the NFL Draft. As it settled in that I really was drafted, I thought about that kid throwing rocks up in the air, hitting 'em with a broomstick, pretending I was Willie Mays. I thought about throwing rocks, hunting with rocks, throwing no-hitters in Little League. I thought about dad telling everyone who would listen that I would have a quarter-million dollar arm someday. I chased a dream since I was 7-years-old and my dream came true.

After I talked to mom and dad, celebrated with my friends and talked to some reporters, I went to Schmitty's office. He had a big smile on his face when I walked in. He stood up, gave me a hug and told me, "Kid, you're going to have the world by the tail. You're good-looking, you're strong. You're the best quarterback I've ever seen."

"You really think so, Schmitty?"

"You'll see," he said.

CHAPTER FOUR

California swagger

I was being recruited by every agent in the business. At the All Star games, agents came at me in waves. I didn't know what to think. They all made promises. There wasn't a lot of regulation, basically anyone could be an agent. They told me I could trust them. Mark McCormick visited me more than any other agent, coming to Santa Clara several times to talk about all the different ways his company could secure my future. I told him what I told all the agents. I want to retire a millionaire. McCormick was impressive because he was as famous as the athletes he was representing. He was doing things a lot of agents would not or could not do. He founded a company called International Management Group and talked a lot about marketability and using athletes to endorse clothing, watches, beverages, sports products. Mark took me to Pebble Beach for the Bing Crosby Pro-Am in the early-spring to recruit me and meet some of his clients. I walked into his hotel suite and there were Arnold Palmer and Jack Nicklaus fixing cocktails at the bar. They came up to me just like regular guys and we talked about golf, football, whatever. I was blown away. IMG had everybody who was anybody and seemed to have big plans for all their clients, and a specific plan ready for me. They wanted 25-percent of my earnings. I thought, "That's an awful lot."

I thought about all my options. I didn't want to hurt anyone's feelings–especially dad, who assumed he was going to represent me. Early in the summer, I decided not to go with IMG–that 25-percent scared me off. Instead, I went with my brother-in-law, Stan House.

Stan had pulled me aside a several times during and after the season, telling me I needed an attorney more than an agent or my dad.

"I know what your dad's thinking. He'll have your best interest at heart. But you really need legal advice. I want what's best for you, too. I'll represent you for free."

I trusted Stan. When we told dad that Stan was going to represent me, it turned into an ugly shouting match. Dad asked me why I didn't trust him. He started yelling that he couldn't believe I was doing this. It got ugly. I shouted back at him, telling him I just wanted to make the smart business decision. I finally just stormed out to my car and mom followed me out.

"Mom, all I wanted was to make you guys proud. I don't want this. I don't need this."

Dad just wanted to protect me. He was not a well-educated man, but he was an honest man. As soon as I made the decision, I was riddled with guilt. I felt like I let down dad, like I put a spike in his heart. I felt like I let the entire family down.

While Stan worked on getting a contract done with the Oilers, the next few weeks for me became a blur. I met with Ed Hughes, King Hill and John Breen. I knew it was a tough and interesting time for the Oilers. I was going into a situation where the team hadn't won, there was a first-year head coach with Hughes and a first-year General Manager in John Breen. It didn't matter to me.

I had that California swagger. I always was confident that I could sling it, lead the team and we'd win. I thought we were going to win the Super Bowl. That's the attitude I had. I was going to show these guys they made the right choice. Even though Ed Hughes made it clear nothing was going to be given to me just because I was the No. 1 pick, I knew I'd win the job if I worked. And I definitely was going to work. Charley Johnson was the incumbent starting quarterback and was a popular player among fans and teammates. Jerry Rhome was in camp, too, and Lynn Dickey was drafted in the third-round out of Kansas State. I didn't blame the Oilers for drafting another quarterback behind me. I mean, I'd been hurt the whole time at Santa Clara. I would have done it, too.

For mini-camp, we stayed at a hotel near the training facility at Fannin and Braeswood, near the Houston Medical Center. I started looking for an apartment. I met Bud Adams, the owner. I did a lot of media interviews. I was pulled in a lot of different directions. Finally, Stan told me we finally reached an agreement on a contract.

The deal was for $250,000 for six years, including a $100,000 bonus, which actually was a loan that I had to pay back in 1980. When Stan told me about the contract, I thought, "I'll be damned. Dad was right. I have a quarter-million dollar arm."

The night before the press conference officially introducing me to Houston, one of the veteran receivers, Mac Haik, took me out and introduced me to everyone on the team. I also went out to some clubs and bars and met a bunch of sponsors and fans. By the end of the night I was three-sheets to the wind. Everybody was buying me drinks. I got home about 3 a.m., and the next morning Lynn Dickey and I were introduced together. It was clear we were on an even playing field and had to fight it out for a job. They liked Dickey. I liked Dickey, too. He had a great arm.

Training camp was at Schreiner Institute in Kerrville, Tx., but I missed about a week of it. I was invited to play in the College All Star Game against the Baltimore Colts, who beat the Cowboys in the previous season's Super Bowl. We played at Soldier Field against the world champs. I was going to be on the same field as Plunkett. That College All Star team included John Brockington, Mike Adamle, Jack Youngblood, Jack Ham, Jack Tatum. Blanton Collier was our coach and he was a legend. He was retiring from the game after 43-years of coaching, including winning a championship in Cleveland.

I had a real good week of practice and Coach Collier had us looking like a pretty good team of All Stars. My teammates voted me captain. I threw the ball real strong, hit receivers perfectly, punted, kicked. I had a hell of a week. The day before the game, though, Coach Collier pulled me aside.

"You're gonna be a great pro, Pastorini. You have all the talent in the world. But I don't know how to tell you this. I've been informed that Plunkett has to start. I've been in this game a long time and no one's ever told me who to start. But there's some politics here."

The game's organizers told Coach Collier that they wanted the Heisman winner to start the game. I didn't even get upset. I expected it, actually. Once I got into the game, I played well and we gave the Super Bowl champs a tough game, losing just 24-17.

On the way to join my teammates, I met with Stan about how he planned to handle my paychecks and investments.

"I don't want to know about it," I told him. "I'm going to be trying to win a job here. I want to play football. I want you to handle my money. I'll trust you."

We agreed that Stan would handle investments and I would get an allowance of $500 after my bills were paid.

"I want to be a millionaire when I retire," I told him.

Once I joined my teammates at Schreiner Institute, I got a chance to settle in and compete with Charley Johnson and Jerry Rhome. They really didn't have the arm strength that Dickey and I had. All the reporters and a lot of my teammates had heard about my arm. On the first day of practice, they wanted to see me throw and watch Jerry Levias run under it. He was the fastest guy on the team. He was a lightning bolt. We lined up for the first scrimmage play and I told Levias, "Run a go."

He took off like a blur. I dropped seven steps. I reached back and threw it out there as long, high and hard as I could, like I was throwing rocks over the restaurant back home. Like I was throwing a ball over Swig Hall. I mean, I slung it. And I over-shot him by about ten yards.

Levias got back to the huddle, shook his head and said, "Nobody's ever done that before."

I smiled, winked, looked him dead in the eyes and said, "Well, get used to it. I'm here. Run faster."

Levias busted out laughing. I knew his story. I knew he'd been through a lot, being the first black player in the Southwest Conference and all the great plays he had made. I think he liked that I just came in with a confident attitude and wasn't intimidated by the league and didn't act any different around black players.

A lot of players in the early-'70s started off kind of unsure about how their relationship with black players would be. There were cliques, some white players didn't like hanging around black players and some black players didn't like hanging around white players. That was just life in the South, but it wasn't me. All the black players and I hit it off pretty good right off the bat. I think that helped me earn some respect in the locker-room and helped me bridge some of the uncertainty between white players on the team and black players.

George Webster wound up being my roommate in Kerrville and took me in, showed me the ropes of the NFL. I had a good camp and was comfortable in Kerrville. It was a lot like Sonora, except a lot hotter. It was a very small town, a cow town, and everyone took us in like family.

When we broke camp, Charley Johnson still was the starting quarterback, but Dickey and I were battling for the spot behind him. Rhome moved on and wound up getting picked up by the Rams. I may not have had the job when I got to Houston, but I did have a fiancé. Pat Heath and I had a whirlwind romance. I proposed to her less than six-months after I met her.

Pat came and stayed with me a lot at the Yorktown Apartments, not far from the Galleria area of Houston. I was cocky, had a little money in my pocket and the town was clamoring for me and Dickey. It was an ongoing competition. Fans and folks in the media took up sides–Are you a Pastorini fan or a Dickey fan? The first home preseason game was against the Chicago Bears at the Astrodome. I got the ovation of a lifetime. Jogging out to the field, I thought, "Man, they love me."

When I lined up for the first play, I looked to the left, looked to the right and then looked out in front of me. There was Dick Butkus. He was frothing at the mouth. There was snot coming out of his nose and he starts yelling at me, "You fucking rookie! I'm gonna rip your head off! You got that rookie?"

I looked him dead in the eye, smiled and said, "Enjoy the view, Dick, that's as close as you're getting to me all night."

I could feel my offensive linemen squirming in front of me, like, "Ah, shit, don't make him mad."

I took the snap on the first play, handed it off and Dick came in and knocked the shit out of me, pushing me down as he stood up after the play. It didn't matter what defense was called, on the next two plays, Dick did the same thing. He knocked the hell out of me. After the third play, he stepped on my chest, spit, then said, "Fucking rook."

I looked up and said, "Yessir, Mr. Butkus," then got into punt formation and booted the ball to them. Nobody said anything, but when we got to the sideline, I could tell some of my teammates were wondering why the hell a quarterback–a rookie–would challenge someone like Butkus. I didn't know why, actually. I didn't know if it was balls, or showing off, or I just had to say something because I just wasn't wired to back down from someone.

We opened the regular-season against Cleveland. It took about an hour for me to realize we probably weren't going to the Super Bowl. We went down 17-0 in the first half and wound up losing 31-0. I didn't play in that game. Dickey did. I stepped in for Johnson in the second game against Kansas City and did pretty well, but didn't play much again until we were 0-3-1 and I got my first start against Detroit. The fans were clamoring for the young guys. They wanted either Lynn or I and they got me, against Detroit. Joe Schmidt and the boys were notorious for blitzing making life miserable on quarterbacks. They had Dick LeBeau, Lem Barney, Mike Lucci. They beat us, but we battled them pretty good. Between the adrenalin, getting pounded and not hydrating well enough, I lost 17-pounds in the game. After the game, my entire body just buckled. My hamstring, quad and both my calves just all locked up with cramps. I had to be helped out of the locker-room, but we wound up at the Marriott Braeswood after the game and guys just started pouring beer down me. I was pouring salt into the beer, too. I must have drunk three pitchers of beer that night, but it was the veterans' way of accepting me into the club. Kenny Houston complimented my passing. Mike Tilleman, one of our big defensive tackles, sat down across the table from me, poured me a beer and said, "Hey, rook, good job today. You've got balls. You took an ass-kicking, but hung in there."

For me that was like winning the game. It was the first time a vet even acknowledged me as an equal. What a feeling. I played well in a close loss the next week at Pittsburgh, then got the first win at home against Cincinnati. I was working my way into a leadership role and building a good rapport with Coach Hughes. There was that constant looking over your shoulder, with nothing earned yet, because Dickey was in the mix. We went back and forth a bit. There were some people who liked me and some who liked him. We both were getting beat up behind our offensive line. I was hurting, anxious about the job and not getting enough sleep. I wanted to be fresh for the next trip to Cincinnati, so before a 5 p.m. meeting the day before playing the Bengals, I asked our trainer Warren Ariail if he had anything to help me sleep. Warren was an old Marine, with a big cigar in his mouth all the time. He gave me a couple of pills that looked like Alka-Seltzer.

"What the hell are these?"

"The big 7-1-4, Dante," Warren told me. "Methaquaalone 714. Take those, you'll be ready to sleep after the movie."

I was ready to fall into a coma before the meeting even began. I couldn't sit up in my chair. I kept literally sliding out of it like I was made out of Jell-O. I couldn't keep my head up without resting my chin in my hands. I about passed out before the movie, guys were looking at me like they'd never seen me quite that drunk before.

The next day I still was woozy before the game. I couldn't shake out of it during warm-ups. I splashed water on my face, drank coffee. I was woozy the entire first-half. Somebody told me one of those pills was about the same strength as 20 Valium. I didn't sober up until halftime, when we already were down 21-3. We wound up losing 28-13.

That was my introduction to some of the goodies in the Candy Store that lined the top of Warren's training room. There were glass jars the size of milk jugs, rows of them, across the entire wall on one side of the room. Valdoxan were the happy pills. Then there were Percocet, which we called red-and-yellows. Black Mollies were Amphetamines. There were pills of every color. I had no idea what some of them were. I just knew you could grab a handful whenever you wanted.

The Quaaludes jar would be empty every day. Guys were just beat up and hurting and needed them to sleep. They'd take them out of the jars by the handful. And what they didn't take, they were selling in bars and nightclubs. Those things were worth some pretty good money. When we went out to party, we had a free source right there in the training room of whatever we wanted, whenever we wanted.

I got familiar with the Candy Store pretty quickly. I was getting the hell beat out of me. But by the last four games of the season, I was playing pretty good and earned the starting job. After the Quaalude game in Cincinnati, we played the hell out of the Browns, then ended the year with three-straight wins against the Steelers, Bills and Chargers. I was becoming the savior in Houston and everyone was talking about Dante Pastorini. With Pat in and out of town, I was enjoying the girls, too. It didn't take me long to figure out the engagement with Pat would not last, but it came to an abrupt end just before the season ended.

Sandy Roberts, my old college girlfriend, was in Dallas for a Miss Teenage America event and came to Houston to visit me. She always called me, "Booga."

I answered my phone one day and heard her sweet voice, "Booga, I'm coming in for a surprise visit."

I enjoyed Sandy's kinds of surprises, so she wound up staying at my apartment for a while. Then, she stayed a while longer. One morning as I was getting ready to head to the training facility, there was a knock at the door. My fiancé Pat decided to come in for a surprise visit, too. As I opened the door, Sandy walked out of my bedroom wearing a bath robe. I looked at Pat standing in the doorway. Then I looked at Sandy.

"Sandy, meet Pat. Pat, that's Sandy. I'll talk to ya'll later, I've got practice."

And I walked out, closing the door behind me. When I got home that afternoon, Pat and Sandy were on the couch, talking. They wound up getting drunk together at my place, comparing notes about how no good an S.O.B. I was and how I never would commit to a real, long-lasting relationship. Sandy decided it was best that Pat and I end our relationship. Pat agreed. So Sandy stayed a while, then a few weeks later, she decided to move on, too.

My best football relationship didn't last, either. Bud Adams fired Ed Hughes after the 1971 season. I couldn't believe Bud would do that, considering Ed coached just one year and we'd won our last three games.

Ed put his neck on the line to draft me and I thought he was doing a lot of good things to help the team grow. The day he got fired, the media called me at my apartment to get a reaction. I was livid.

"What do I think about Ed getting fired? I think it's wrong. Why don't you go ask Mr. Adams if every well that he drills hits oil? Go ask him if every investment he makes pays off in one year. How can you judge a man in one year?"

The reporters loved it. Here was this hotshot rookie, ripping his owner. They called me things like precocious. It embarrassed Bud Adams, but I was loyal to Ed Hughes and of course I was going to tell you what I thought.

A couple of days later, Bud Adams made me issue an apology. I told reporters I overstepped my boundaries. I said Mr. Adams was the owner and he knew what he was doing. It was all bullshit.

The fact is, Bud didn't know what he was doing. I didn't even really know Bud as a man. All I knew is I only saw him when I signed my contract and whenever we won he would come into the locker-room three-sheets to the wind. He was a different kind of man. He just wasn't the kind of guy you could build a relationship with. He showed us off a lot like part of a gun collection, or a stable of horses or something. He took Dickey and me up to Judge Roy Hofheinz's suite in the Astrodome one night, parading us around in front of all his old River Oaks friends. It was like, "look at these two guys I own." Dickey and I just shook hands, had a couple of drinks and moved along.

It was a huge mistake firing Ed. We were just starting to mesh. John Breen, as it turned out, wanted to wield some power as general manager, so he rammed one of his cronies down Bud's throat as the next coach. I don't know how he thought Bill Petersen could coach or lead an NFL team, because he couldn't. Everyone knew Petersen was a mistake as soon as Bud hired him. Some of the veterans knew about Petersen's reputation and it spread pretty quickly that this guy knew nothing about professional football. He was a college coach from Florida State and spent 1971 just down the road from the Astrodome at Rice. Somehow, Peterson convinced Breen and Bud Adams to fire Hughes. It took me about five minutes being around him in the off-season to realize Petersen was the biggest idiot that ever walked the face of the earth. When he talked in a meeting, we looked at each other in the locker-room like, "What the fuck did he just say?"

The guy couldn't put two sentences together. And this was the guy that was supposed to lead us to the promised land of the playoffs.

CHAPTER FIVE

"Hold the sideline under your right arm."

When the 1972 season began, there no longer was any question the Oilers were my team. Charley Johnson moved on to Denver. Jerry Rhome was in Los Angeles. And my backup, Lynn Dickey, suffered one of the ugliest injuries I'd ever seen. In a pre-season game, against the St. Louis Cardinals, Dickey scrambled and was dragged to the Astrodome turf from behind. His knee jammed into his hip socket so hard, the socket shattered, breaking bones and tearing ligaments. He was in agonizing pain on the field. I mean, agonizing. Doctors snapped Dickey's leg back into socket on the field and we all knew it would be at least a year, if ever, before Dickey would be the same again. Even as he was getting carted off, trainers and doctors on the sideline were saying things like he may never walk again–it was that bad. That's the reality of the game. I watched Dickey writhing in pain and realized, like every player did at some point, I'm that close to being in the same spot. Especially considering my new head coach was a buffoon and my offensive line had changed completely from the season before, I knew I was going to have to stand up to a lot of punishment.

I engaged in some preventive medication a number of ways. Going out and drinking, partying, picking up girls and having a good time really was a kind of self-medicating thing for me. The football environment was so controlled and rigid at Fannin and Braeswood, it wore us down physically. Coach Peterson wore us down mentally. The intensity level was so fierce, every time we got a break from meetings, practice and working out, we made the most of it. We cut loose. And there wasn't a better place in the league to cut loose than Houston, Tx. I arrived to Houston when it was on the cusp of exploding with energy—literally. Oil practically ran down the streets. The city was a lot like me, or I was a lot like the city. It was growing up fast, flexing muscles and was untamed. You could see it and feel it all over town. By 1972, population had more than doubled in the city. People from every corner of the country were coming to Houston for work and there was plenty of work to go around. It was an amazing time. Money literally came through the Ship Channel every day, tankers and ships barreling in and out of the Port Of Houston with millions of gallons of oil, gas and everything related to the oil and gas industries. NASA brought all kinds of attention and jobs, as did the Astrodome—the so-called, Eighth Wonder Of The World. The oil and gas industries couldn't keep up with demands. If someone picked up and moved from Ohio or Michigan one week, they'd have a job and as much work as they wanted by the next week. The biggest shopping mall in the country opened, The Galleria. Skyscrapers were popping up all over downtown. Blue-collar workers were just like us NFL players. They'd work a double-shift three straight days, pack as much work as they could into as many hours as they could stand, then roll into town with wads of bills in their pockets ready to party. The white-collar traders were up before dawn, traded all day and then hit Happy Hour, dropping cash everywhere. There were women everywhere.

They were beautiful women and there was just something about Houston women. They reflected the same kind of ambitious, outrageous, untamed style as everyone else. Strip malls and restaurants opened at the blink of an eye. Housing developments popped up overnight: The Woodlands, Lake Conroe, Clear Lake. Strip clubs, honky tonks and night clubs kept the same pace. Bars and restaurants overflowed with partiers, socialites, cowboys, oilfield workers, energy executives, NASA folks.

It was football country with attitude and an unlimited budget. And I was the 23-year-old quarterback from a town of 1,300 people, turned loose in one of the biggest, fastest-growing cities in the country. What was a red-blooded Italian-American to do? Everybody knew me. I was the saving grace. Everybody was my buddy. Everybody loved me. And I ate it up. I started getting intoxicated by all the fame and attention. I started getting intoxicated, period. Everyone wanted a piece of me. Everyone wanted to get me into some kind of business deal. Every girl I met, it seemed, wanted to get me into bed. I was living the dream.

When we opened the season in Denver against the Broncos I felt like everything was about to break wide open for me and the Oilers. It was a highly anticipated game by the networks and across the country. NFL Films showed up, because the game featured Denver's John Ralston, the first-year coach from Stanford, against Peterson, who was supposed to be an offensive genius from Florida State. Of course, every guy in the locker-room knew Petersen didn't know shit, but fans and media all bought into it. That first game was featured nationally, partly also because of the hotshot quarterback that played for Houston. I thought it would be a good launching point for a breakout season. In the locker-room just before the game, Petersen gathered us all together. I sat at my locker, some other guys sat alongside at their lockers on both sides of me. The rest of the team surrounded Petersen on a knee or sitting on the floor. Everyone was nervous, quietly fidgeting, going through the usual pre-game routine. Some guys closed their eyes and focused, others stared off blankly, or bowed their heads going over assignments or alone in their thoughts. Then, coach Pete gave us the season-opening pregame speech.

"Men," he barked at us, "I want you to think about one word. This entire season is going to be about one word and one word only. That's all we're thinking about this year. Every day, remember one word. Everything is about one word. And that word is, 'Super Bowl.'"

I said under my breath, "Well, coach, that's two words, but OK. I'm still with you."

He went on, with a few guys raising their eyebrows over the "one word" comment.

"Now when you go out there for the National Anthem, I want you all to make sure you stand on your helmets and hold the sideline under your right arm."

Across the room you could see guys starting to tremble and snicker under their breath. I looked at Charlie Joiner and Kenny Burrough. They turned their heads away, trying not to laugh in Petersen's face. Guys were biting their lips, whispering to each other, "Is this fucking guy serious? THIS is our coach?"

Petersen then told us, "Now everybody grab a knee so I can lead you in the Lord's Prayer."

We all bowed our heads and Petersen began.

"Now I lay me down to sleep . . . ah, shit, fuck, no, that's not it. Now I lay . . . Ah, shit . . . Pastorini!! You're Catholic. You lead us!"

Everybody in the locker-room started just dying, shaking, tears rolling down guys' faces. I had to pause to keep from laughing out loud as I knelt at the middle of the room, covered my face with one hand and said the prayer, "Our Father, who art in Heaven . . ."

By the time I finished, some guys had put socks in their mouths, trying not to laugh out loud. We ran out of the locker-room in front of the coaches and busted out laughing. As we went through the tunnel, Broncos fans looked at us like, man, that's a loose team.

Before we even took the first snap of our first game, we realized that poor son-of-a-bitch Petersen had no clue. We got killed. We lost 30-17 and I got the shit kicked out of me. The NFL Films crew kept putting the camera on Petersen and he kept acting like he had it all under control

"Hey, ref. Ref!" he shouted at one point when I got buried by a rushing defensive player. "You know, that kid's got parents!"

What did that have to do with anything? Our left tackle, Gene Ferguson, missed a couple of blocks in a row and I got pounded by defenders. When Ferguson walked off the field, Petersen saw the cameras and yelled at Ferguson, "I'm not going to take this standing down!"

Ferguson stopped, stared Petersen in the face and said, "Standing up, coach? Or lying down?"

We put up with that kind of shit all year long. It was a disaster. Petersen was in way over his head. Our personnel were overwhelmed and under-coached.

On the first play of the game against Pittsburgh a few weeks later, I got speared from behind and broke three Transverse Processes in the middle of my back. I played the whole game, but it was just a constant beating I took. I never said a word about the offensive line, because I never wanted to hang a teammate out to dry. Really, it wasn't completely their fault. Breen acquired sub-par players and Petersen put them in an impossible situation. Fans turned quickly on us—especially me.

We did beat the Jets and Joe Namath in a huge upset the third week of the season, when Joe and I got into a good old-fashioned passing war. I looked forward to that game and enjoyed it. I wanted to really show up strong against Joe Willie. He was the guy with the target on his chest and, like always, I wanted to go head-to-head against the best. We picked them apart. I threw for 278-yards and a touchdown. We beat them, 26-20.

The next week I had the worst game of my life. It was one that shook my soul, more so for what happened after the game than during it. We played the Raiders on Monday Night Football.

I was horrible. I couldn't get out from under center without getting hit and just played badly. I went 3-for-21 passing and threw four interceptions. Three of the interceptions were by defensive linemen, who batted down at least 10 balls in my face. They were all over me, all night. The fourth was picked by linebacker Phil Villapiano on the Raiders goal-line and I had to run him down 80-yards to keep him from scoring. We lost 34-0. Late in the game, as Frank Gifford, Don Meredith and Howard Cosell were trying to find something to talk about as we embarrassed ourselves, the ABC cameras turned to a pissed-off Oilers fan, who saw the camera and shot the finger on national television. The game was remembered for Meredith quipping, "He thinks they're No. 1."

It was the ugly side of pissed-off fans that stuck with me. When I walked into the Astrodome parking lot after the game, I saw my car, a black Lincoln Continental with "Oilers 7" vanity license plates had been vandalized. There were key-mark scratches all the way across both sides of the car. The headlight lenses were ripped off and thrown to the ground. Both mirrors were broken. There was some kind of message scratched onto the hood of the car. All four tires were slashed.

I was mad, of course. I wanted to find the S.O.B.s that did that to my car and kick their asses. But more than anything I was hurt. I started questioning myself. Is it me? Is it the team? Am I not good? I always played it cool and took the heat publicly, because I knew that's what it took to be a leader. But I also heard all the comments and nicknames: Dan "Pass-to-the-other-teamy" was one. Fans piled on. For a guy that–quote, unquote–had it all, I doubted myself an awful lot. That Monday night game woke me up. I knew I could be a target anytime, anywhere. I began carrying a gun in my car.

The next week after practice, I had a long talk with the person I respected the most in the organization, King Hill.

"What am I doing wrong, coach? Is it me? Tell me what I need to do."

He told me, "It's not your fault. We're going to get you help. It'll happen."

We never won another game in '72. Late in the year we went to San Diego, where my mom watched me play football for the first time. When I was a kid and while at Santa Clara, dad always went on the football trips, while mom watched the restaurant. She also didn't want to see me get hurt. The Chargers game did nothing to ease her nerves. I was knocked out of the game four times, including once with a concussion. Trainers and doctors dragged me off the field four times, but every time I talked my way back onto the field. I wanted mom to see me do something special. Deacon Jones was shredding through the line, though, tossing me around, stomping on me, spearing me. Every time I got knocked out, I told the trainers and coaches, "You don't understand. I have to play. My mother's in the stands."

But every time I went back in, I only seemed to get hit more. When I threw the ball, I got knocked in the ribs. When I handed off, I got driven into the dirt. I was sacked just twice, but got the piss knocked out of me all day. Deacon Jones terrorized our offensive line. He didn't give a damn about quarterbacks, but even he, after crushing me on a play, pointed to Peterson on our sideline and yelled, "Get this kid out of here before I kill him."

Mom told me after the game that she'd never watch me play again.

The last straw for me as far as Petersen was concerned came in the last game against Cincinnati. I got hurt at Pittsburgh the week before. We played the hell out of the Steelers, who were on their way to winning their first division title. We hung in there and lost, 9-3, but I had to be helped off the field after the game. I played with three fractures of the transverse processes in my back. I also had a couple of broken fingers and busted my nose pretty good during the game. They started my backup Kent Nix against the Bengals, but I suited up. We totally quit as a team. Everyone half-assed it and the Bengals kicked the hell out of us. With about two minutes left in the game, we were losing 61-10. Poor Nix was getting pummeled all day and finally went down.

With Nix knocked out of the game, I walked over to the third-teamer, Ed Baker and began going over a few things with him. I told him to get rid of the ball quickly, don't get hurt, just make simple plays. But Peterson walked up to me instead. He stood in front of me and leaned in to whisper in my ear.

"Can you play, Dan?"

I thought to myself, what the hell? Is this guy serious? We're losing 61 to 10 and he wants me to play? I thought, OK, I'll play along with your little nonsense. I leaned in toward him and spoke softly into Petersen's ear.

"So, coach. What do you want me to do? Should I tie it up or pull it out?"

Then, I just lost it.

"Don't even think about putting my ass out there. Are you kidding me? I've played hurt all season. I don't miss games. I've put up with this shit all damn season. And you want me to go out there in a 61-10 game?"

Petersen walked away and put Baker in for the rest of the game.

Nobody in the locker room respected Peterson. He was a joke and we were an NFL punch-line. Bud Adams had to fire the guy. Even though I would be on my third head coach in three years, I was willing to make that trade if it meant getting rid of Coach Pete. But, nope. Adams announced he would bring Petersen back for another season. I actually wondered if it was too late to call the Mets. It really was so bad I wondered if I could go back to baseball and get away from this mess.

After the season, I went back to California to see mom and dad. We had our Christmas with the family, so I saw Stan and Dorothy. I asked him about the investment he made with my $100,000 bonus.

"I've got some bad news. That investment didn't work out."

I asked Stan, "How bad is it?"

"We've lost it all."

I slumped into my chair. "What the hell happened?"

"Don't worry, we'll make it back."

I told Stan, "With what?"

None of it made sense to me, especially when I received some confusing documents from the IRS. There were red flags everywhere. I hired Sam Cohen, an attorney out of San Jose, to investigate what Stan did with the money I gave him to invest. Sam called just a few days later and told me Stan and Dorothy had invested the money and he believed they stole from me.

"Dan, this guy sold you down the river. That thing made a boatload of money."

Stan apparently built an office strip-center in Morgan Hill not far from San Jose. It was apparent he put the investments in my sister's name. But the loan was in my name. I paid the loan, they made the money. After Sam investigated it more, I confronted Stan at mom and dad's house.

"What did you do with the money?"

He looked nervous.

"I'm getting mom and dad in here, because I want everyone to know what a scumbag you are."

Sam Cohen stood up and got in Stan's face.

"You are a disgrace to our profession. There are people who take advantage of others, but you took advantage of family. I could send you to jail. I could put you under the jail."

Sam went through the whole thing in front of my parents. I turned to dad, "Are you hearing this? This is the scumbag your daughter married."

Stan couldn't say a word. He was shaking, holding a cigarette in his hand and couldn't even smoke it, he was shaking so much. My sister was just as guilty.

Sam told me, "I could make sure this guy never practices law again. Is that what you want?"

I was numb trying to figure out why my sister did this to me. I was her brother. Her blood. Money meant more to them than blood and it hurt very deep. Just a few weeks before, I flew their kids to Houston, put them up at my house, paid for everything they wanted and took them to games to see me play. The whole time, my sister and brother-in-law were stealing from me. Stan was a scoundrel; a skunk. But I decided not to go after him, because his kids adored me, and it would kill mom and dad for me to tear apart Dorothy's family with a lawsuit.

All I asked for was five minutes in the room, alone, with Stan.

Stan thought I was going to kill him. But all I wanted was for him to be looking over his shoulder for the rest of his life. I wanted him to always think about how he broke apart the family, hurt my parents and hurt me. I wanted to scare the hell out of him.

I stood close in front of Stan and stared him square in the face.

"You son of a bitch. Remember this: The minute mom and dad die, I'll have your ass."

CHAPTER SIX

No more patience

Not long after I got back to Houston, I was at home watching The Tonight Show, when Johnny Carson had animal trainer Jim Fowler as a guest. Johnny asked Fowler, "What is the most deceptive animal in the world?"

Fowler answered, "You mean other than man?"

How profound. After discovering what Stan and Dorothy did to me, I was confused, mad and never felt more isolated. I didn't know whom to trust anymore. Fans had turned on me, vandalizing my car. Coach Petersen had the franchise going nowhere. I couldn't trust my own family. I couldn't trust women, business people, friends. If there was money involved, I felt as if everybody could turn on me. The irony was I really didn't have a lot of money. I made a decent living, but Stan and Dorothy stole $100,000 and my salary wasn't much by quarterback standards. The only other investment I ever made was with Marty Sammons. I gave him $2,500 to just shut up. Marty was a friend of a friend who pestered me about some kind of stock deal he was getting into. I finally just gave him $2,500 and told him to leave me alone. Everybody thought I was a rich man, but I wasn't. It was difficult even getting a car loan. When I applied for a loan, banks questioned my long-term earnings potential and made getting loans difficult. I also was riddled with guilt again over going against my dad's wishes in the first place when I signed with Stan. Dad would have protected me and had he said, "Hey, Willie, I'm going to take a little of this for me," then at least I would have known. Dad never would have stolen from me like my brother-in-law. After I fired Stan, I hired Tommy Vance from Beaumont as my agent. King Hill recommended him and Tommy was close to Houston, so I knew he would be plugged into things with the Oilers. My contract wasn't due to expire for another couple of years, but I needed someone who knew the league, knew the Oilers and could help me with some off-field opportunities. Tommy represented Alex Karras, who had retired from the Lions and was beginning an acting career.

One of the first things Tommy got me into was a made-for-TV competition on ABC Sports between NFL quarterbacks. The network brought in Jim Plunkett, Archie Manning, Roger Staubach, Terry Bradshaw, Bob Griese, all the big names of the era. We competed in various tests, including throwing a football for distance. When I was coming out of college, I heard some scouts and coaches say they'd never seen a stronger arm than mine, but I didn't take it very seriously. I just figured they were going a little over the top. The ABC contest was in Miami and they had various tests for us, like throwing at moving targets on golf carts, running in one direction or the other, running through an obstacle course. Then we lined up one-by-one and threw a football for distance. Each quarterback threw the football as far as they could from the goal-line on one end of the Orange Bowl. Before I stepped up, Bradshaw threw the ball 65-yards, which was the longest throw of the day. I grabbed a football, took three steps and slung the ball as high and long as I could, just like the old days at home or Swig

Hall. The ball hit on the opposite 13-yard-line. It went 87-yards in the air. When the ball hit the ground, I just started laughing, I couldn't believe it. The TV guys screamed and hollered and the other quarterbacks just shook their heads. Griese followed me and he was the last quarterback to throw. He was hilarious, knowing he had no shot to get close to Bradshaw, much less me. He ran toward the goal-line and then just kept running. He ran past the 10-yard-line, still holding the football. He ran past the 20-, 30—and when he got to the 50-yard line, finally tossed the ball out where my ball landed. Bradshaw told me he'd never seen a ball thrown further than my 87-yarder. Someone on the ABC team told me it was the longest recorded throw in history.

I was proud of it. I always was proud of my arm strength. Then the reality hit that Staubach, Bradshaw and Griese were going back to the Cowboys, Steelers and Dolphins. I was going back to a mess.

The only promising thing about 1973 was Sid Gillman came in as general manager and was hands-on in every way. Sid knew football, especially offense. For the third consecutive season, my entire offensive line changed. Some of those poor guys who blocked for me couldn't hit their asses with both hands. It was bad. Sid was the only glimmer of hope I had left.

He brought in the vertical passing game. Sid was all about stretching the field, going through progressions and timing throws and receivers making precise cuts. It was stuff that a lot of NFL teams had never before seen. From the first day of camp, Sid taught me things about the passing game that I didn't know, and I was a guy who prided myself on knowing the game and exploiting the chess game in offensive football.

Sid's only problem was he was the biggest jerk with whom I ever dealt. He had no people skills. He jumped players' shit, embarrassed them. I never had that type of coach before. With my temper, I didn't respond well to the stuff Sid was shoveling. No one ever coddled me and I didn't want anyone coddling me, but from the time I had John Hannah in high school, to Pat Malley at Santa Clara, to even Ed Hughes and certainly King Hill, the coaches that treated me like a man were the ones that got the most out of me and were the ones I respected the most. If I screwed up a play, King would look me in the eye and say, "Hey, come on, you're better than that. Do it this way. Try it again."

King expected a lot and corrected me, but he would do it away from the team and he would work with you. Gillman just yelled. It was an interesting balance and relationship we had. Sid knew his stuff and I reached a point during camp when I decided to just do what he told me and ignore his abrasive style. I mean, I hadn't won in three years and I was hungry to win. If this was what it took to get to where I wanted to go, OK, let's go down this road.

Sid was a freak about filming practices and going over the tapes. He filmed everything. He had someone hold a camera between my legs to film how I received the snap. He put a camera overhead to see the progressions I was making from my point of view. He filmed me from the defensive point of view, moving left-to-right and right-to-left. He filmed from behind the line-of-scrimmage, to see my throwing points on the run. He had so many subtle pointers and gave me a lot of good drills. Sid really helped me and taught me. He just wasn't the best guy to be around. I didn't like it, but I believed. I bought in. Sid worked our asses off in camp, but those of us that had been around a couple years had faith that we'd finally win.

We didn't. Peterson was just overwhelmed. Two games and two losses into the 1973 season, Sid took over all the meetings. Gilman basically was the head coach, while Bill was just a beaten man, a shell of a man. Any time we met, Bill sat in a chair in the back-corner of the room, slumped over almost in a fetal position. It was sad. We all thought, why don't you just quit and go away? Or fire the man and let him have a little dignity. As much as we hated the guy, we really felt sorry for him, the way he was humiliated and emasculated. He was in over his head and he was not a mentally strong person. Petersen was not mentally fit to be a coach. How the hell he accomplished all that at Florida State was beyond me. Bud finally did Petersen a favor and fired him five-games into the season. We were 0-5.

It didn't make a difference giving Gilman the official title. We had a few decent moments under Sid, but the losing and a losing attitude continued, permeating through the locker-room. Even when we were up in a game, there was a sense on the sideline of, "How the hell are we going to screw this one up?"

And we usually did. In 1971, I was sacked more than any other quarterback in the league. In 1972, I held that record again. In 1973, I was on my way to having that distinction yet again. It literally was depressing. I did a good job of not allowing doubt and my personal insecurities to infect my play on the field, but off the field I was embarrassed and wondered if I'd ever win. At Cincinnati we got beat like a drum. Mike Reid planted me into the ground on one play, then tapped my helmet as he picked me up off the turf and said, "Hang in there, kid, it'll get better."

I just couldn't see it coming anytime soon. The combination of frustration, having a lot of players who didn't belong in the league and getting beaten to a pulp every Sunday had me doubting everything. I also had no real sounding board, no real family or friend that I could trust. I felt isolated.

Bill Curry was my roommate in 1973. Bill was a veteran that I respected and was president of the Player's Association. He and I were captains and I tried to find hope in all the reaffirming conversations we had. Bill was a true leader and a great, great, man. He kept telling me these things can change overnight, that we would have our day soon. But Bill suffered an injury and wasn't around as much later in the year. There was a time bomb ticking inside of me, I was just so frustrated. Here I was three years into my career and while guys like Bradshaw, Staubach, Griese and Ken Stabler were having things fall perfectly into place for them, I was on my way to a second-straight 1-13 season.

I was heckled pretty badly in our second-to-last game at the Astrodome. That bomb inside me went off. I'd had enough. I stood on the sideline as we were getting beat and some guy in the stands just rode my ass. Especially in the second half, he was telling me to give up the game, that I was sorry, to go back to California and that I was a wasted pick. He called me a jackass, a pretty boy, a loser. I was steaming mad. The Raiders kicked our asses and by the time the fourth-quarter wound down, there were less than ten thousand fans in the Astrodome, so a lot of people could hear this jackass riding me.

As the game ended, I watched the clock tick down–five, four, three, two, one–and when the clock hit zero, I turned and sprinted toward the section where the heckler was sitting. I pointed at him and tore into him. I called him every name in the book.

"Alright, you son of a bitch. Call me that shit now. I'll climb up there and beat your ass. Say something now."

I lost it. In front of women, some kids, everybody. Everyone in the stands looked at me, shocked. As I walked away, I pointed to the guy again and kept telling him, "Say something now, asshole. Say something now."

It was clear by the looks on some of the faces in the stands that I lost some fans with my outburst. Worse, a few minutes later in the locker-room, a trainer came up to me and said, "Uh, Dan . . . You know that guy that was heckling you?"

"What about him?"

"They took him out of there right before the game ended."

"What?"

"Yeah, the police came down and took him away because those fans were complaining about him."

Oh, God. Here it was Sunday and all those people went to church, spent their hard-earned money to come watch a bad team play football, and I embarrassed myself in front of them. I didn't even cuss out the right guy.

I lost it again the next week, against Cincinnati in our last game of the year. I was miserable. I went into the Cincinnati game on the verge of back-to-back 1-13 seasons and was just sick of losing. I wasn't going to take it anymore. I had no more patience. By the middle of the third-quarter, I was getting the shit kicked out of me again. Tom Funchess was like an usher out there, letting defensive linemen and linebackers into the backfield. We were losing 27-10 and I got drilled into the turf again–again by Mike Reid. I felt that familiar tingle, sting and wooziness of getting slammed into the artificial turf, which was like concrete. When I got back to the huddle, I told Funchess, "Get out. Get the hell out of my huddle. Tell 'em to send somebody in here who can block."

Funchess bowed up on me and started cussing me out, telling me to get off his case. I told him again, "Get out."

I finally called timeout, went to the sideline and told Sid, "You either get his ass out of there or put someone in for me. I'm tired of this shit."

Sid pulled Funchess and we scored two touchdowns before the Bengals knew what hit 'em. We lost 27-24, but actually showed some life.

After the game, Sid pulled me aside and said, "You know, Dan, you've got to be careful with the black players."

"No, I don't, Sid. I don't have to be careful with the black players. Let me tell you something, the black players like me. I don't treat anyone black or white on this football team and they know that. George Webster was my roommate. There are no black or white players on this team. There are guys who want to play and guys who don't. I don't want to be on the field with guys who don't want to play. The son of a bitch wasn't blocking."

Taking that stand woke up a lot of guys. I could see it in their eyes in the huddle and I could feel it from that point on, at practice and in the locker-room. They realized how much I cared. I wasn't going to take losing anymore. I heard rumors about getting traded and there was a lot of criticism of me all over town. I heard all of it. I always said I didn't care what people said about me, but I did.

The more frustrated I got, the more my temper flared. I yelled. I punctuated most every conversation with some kind of curse word. I screamed and threw things. I sensed everywhere I went that I wasn't the golden boy anymore. I was the quarterback, so I got blamed, but I didn't expect to get targeted.

Not long after the season ended, a friend of mine, Jimmy Hewitt, invited me to go watch some motocross races in a town called Cleveland, northeast of Houston. After watching the races, driving my '73 Pantera back into town, I was pulled over by a motorcycle cop. That Pantera was pretty well known around Houston. It was talked about in the papers, it had been on TV as I drove out of the Astrodome parking lot and I talked about it a few times with reporters, because I loved cars and racing so much. When I pulled off the highway near town, I turned off the car, rolled down the windows and put both my hands on the steering wheel. I wasn't drunk. In fact, I hardly had anything to drink at the races. Jimmy, however, definitely was drunk. When I looked at my rearview mirror, I saw the cop with his gun drawn, signaling for me to get out of the car. I was wearing a t-shirt, cutoff shorts and flip-flops. I just put my hands up and said, "You got the right guy?"

He told me, "Where are you going in such a hurry?"

"I guess I was going a little fast, officer."

He told me he was going to charge me with evading an officer.

"What? What are you talking about? As soon as I saw you, I pulled over."

He said he followed me for several miles and I refused to stop, which was total bullshit. I was handcuffed, arrested and my car was impounded, while a friend took Jimmy home. As soon as we got to the police station, the officer began parading me up and down the hallways, as if to say, "Look who I got." He made sure everybody in the building saw me in handcuffs. We got to the booking room and he announced, yelling, "I got Dan Pastorini!"

That's when I heard another officer–his superior–storm into the room and confront the officer, "What the HELL are you doing? Do you know how much money that kid brings into our force for needy kids? Do you have any idea what he does for our charities; what he does for this city? You got Dan Pastorini for evading? What happened?"

The officer then told his story to his boss, but everybody in the room realized it was a bunch of bull. He got his ass chewed, then came out, apologized to me and let me go with no charges. The guy just wanted a notch on his belt. The incident never even made the papers. No one outside the people in that police station even knew it happened, but it definitely stuck with me. Had the officer in charge not been a fair, reasonable guy, I would have been arrested for something I didn't do–just because some cop wanted to say he got Dan Pastorini. It made me skeptical of law enforcement. It was eye-opening.

I needed something good to happen. It finally did when Anita Martini called and asked if I'd like to go to the premier of a Broadway show that was in town. Anita was a wonderful woman. She was a broadcasting legend in Houston and a pioneer for women journalists. She was fair and well-connected. Her family had a history in theater, so she always knew actors that came into town for shows.

"I'll introduce you to June Wilkinson," Anita told me. "You'll like that."

Who wouldn't like that? June was a striking woman. She was a Playboy icon and was knocking it out of the park on the dinner-theater circuit. Hugh Hefner called her, "The Bosom," with good reason. June's measurements were 43-23-37. She had made seven appearances in Playboy Magazine and became close friends with Hef. Anyone that knew June loved her. She was impossible not to love. She did movies, had a great sense of timing on stage and just drew everyone's eyes toward her. She dated Elvis for a while when she was younger and was friends with Henry Kissinger. She had that kind of range in her personality. I mean, she was a knockout. Jayne Mansfield, Mamie Van Doren and June were the three most sought-after models and pinup girls of their time. When I met June and talked with her at the after-show party, I realized immediately that she may be an uninhibited personality, but June had a real sense of business and marketing. She was smart. I got to know her over the next few weeks and before long we were dating. It was whirl-wind, but we truly swept each other off our feet. She was beautiful, gracious, sexy. Everybody just gawked over her. She did a few movies, but it was on the dinner playhouse circuit where she was a fantastic star, earning top dollar touring across the country. I fell for her and she fell for me. I think as much as anything, June was the first person I'd known in several years that I didn't feel wanted anything from me. She had her own money, her own name and she was sincere. I trusted her. We got married in Carmel, much to the disappointment of a lot of my friends, who all said I shouldn't marry a woman who was nine-years older than me. That's one of the things Tommy Vance and Alex Karras told me–don't do it, don't do it. But I didn't care. I finally found some stability with a beautiful woman who didn't seem to want anything from me. And I wanted a family. June brought me into the world of Hollywood, too. We went to parties all over L.A., where she had a beautiful house. We had an open invitation to Hef's mansion. June talked me into giving acting a shot, too, in a movie she was doing called Florida Connection, which was about drugs and–interestingly—corrupt cops. We shot the movie outside Naples, Fla., so I was with June all summer.

I went to L.A. with Tommy Vance and Alex Karras, who was working on another movie called Blazing Saddles. As we drove to Hollywood, Alex sat in the backseat and read from the script. We laughed so hard I had to pull off the road.

Seeing Hollywood's fantasy world from the inside was exhilarating. Watching June work, traveling with her on the theater circuit, bringing so many thrills to so many fans was exactly what I needed. Unfortunately, I brought June into the world of the NFL, too. Before training camp began for the 1974 season, June and I were at a fine steakhouse in Houston called Brenner's. It was a very nice place, quiet, elegant, upscale in every way. We just wanted a nice dinner together before I would spend most of my time playing football and June would be back and forth doing shows. It was impossible for June and I to go anywhere discreetly. I had a lot of eyes on me everywhere I went, and when I was with June everyone's eyes were on her.

As we sat at our table, a guy two tables away from us started talking about me, making sure he was loud enough for June and me to hear.

"Damn worthless Pastorini," he said. "He can't play football. He's a prima donna California boy. We should cut his ass."

He just kept on and on. It was one thing heckling me in a stadium, or even talking shit about me to your friends at a bar. But this was an upscale restaurant. People were in there having quiet conversations, dressed in suits and ties, the ladies wearing cocktail dresses. And this guy was ripping me a new one? June was incredibly uncomfortable and upset. I grabbed her hands and told her, "Don't let it bother you, baby. Don't worry about it."

She was insulted, embarrassed and pissed off. We finally stood up to leave and the entire restaurant went silent. Everyone apparently heard this asshole heckling me and wondered what I would do. I stopped next to his table, nodded my head to his date as if to say hello, then leaned over and looked him right in the eye.

"You're a coward. Anytime you want to suit up and play my position just say the word. You prick."

CHAPTER SEVEN

Everybody called him Bum

I may not have been the most popular guy in Houston anymore, but I was a hit in Las Vegas. The NFL sponsored a junket to Vegas in the summer of '74. I was stunned when I walked through the casinos. You would have thought I just won back-to-back Super Bowls, rather than finish with consecutive 1-13 seasons. When I first heard pit bosses and dealers shouting my name as I walked through the casino, I thought it was just a few fans from Houston or Northern California who recognized me. But it kept happening. And it happened at more than one casino. I started thinking, "Man, we may not be good, but I'm a superstar." Then it just got strange. I finally asked a dealer why everyone seemed to know me. I got introduced to what football really is all about.

"You guys are legendary. You beat the spread just about every damn game."

I didn't know if it was a compliment or scary, but in the two years we went 1-13, we beat the spread more than 20-times. We lost games, but at least we made Vegas a lot of money. It was mind-blowing how big the NFL was becoming almost overnight. Everything was changing and changing fast. Money was skyrocketing, Monday Night Football turned the league into a ratings monster and the NFL was king of the sports world.

There was a players strike in 1974, but it wasn't much of one. It lasted 42-days. When we got to training camp, Gilman shook things up. On the first day of training camp, Sid stood up and told us, "This isn't a democracy. It's a dictatorship. And I'm the dick."

He then pointed at several players in the room.

"You, you, you, you and you . . . get out of here."

He cut player reps, guys who spoke out during the strike and players he was just tired of carrying on the roster. The atmosphere in the locker-room was changing. Bill Curry was right. Even if the wins didn't happen as fast as I hoped, Sid brought in some young guys on the defensive side of the ball that looked talented. We were going to be young, but guys like Curley Culp and Elvin Bethea were coming into their own on the defensive line. We had young playmakers like Gregg Bingham, Ted Washington and Willie Alexander. Sid also brought in an old high school and college coach to coordinate the defense–O.A. Phillips. Everybody called him Bum. I was working on my fourth different starting offensive line, but finally felt pretty good about the direction the offense was headed and some of the guys that we had at the skill positions. Billy Johnson was a rookie that had some swagger. He was a fast, flamboyant kid and always wore white shoes, like Joe Namath. He gave me nice options, opening up things for my big target–No. 00, Kenny Burrough. I felt as if we finally were going to make some noise and start heading in the right direction.

It didn't look like it would happen when we opened the season 1-5, but we went 6-2 the rest of the way. We won three road games in a row along the way and beat Pittsburgh in Pittsburgh in a game that was an absolute bloodbath. I got beat to hell. Bradshaw got beat to hell. Bum's new three-four alignment on defense was clicking. It was the last game the Steelers lost before winning their first Super Bowl.

The movie I made with June was released late in the season, too. The premiere was in Houston and every power-broker and socialite in town was at the River Oaks Theater to see June and me on the big screen. It was a huge event, women dressed to the hilt and reporters and cameras everywhere. Five minutes into the movie, I was looking for a door to go out or a hole to crawl into. I thought I did pretty well when we filmed the Florida Connection. I thought I read the lines smoothly, but watching myself trying to act made me just cringe. It was an embarrassment. I sounded like a bad middle-school actor: "HI. I. Am. Going. To kill you now." I was horrible.

Still, for the first time in my career, I felt good at the end of a season and I had a lot to feel good about. We easily could have gone 10-4 in the toughest division in football, with the Steelers becoming a dominant team, the Bengals slinging it everywhere with Kenny Anderson and Cleveland's "Cardiac Kids" making noise. After the last game of the year, Sid had champagne in the locker-room for us.

"This is what I want you guys to get used to," Sid told us. "This is what you deserve. Winning."

In the summer, I found out June was pregnant. That's when I met with Sid after the season and asked him to look at my contract. I wanted security. I wanted to make sure I'd always be able to take care of this baby.

"Look, Sid, I'm supposed to make $40,000 this year and some of these linemen that aren't blocking for me make $100,000. That's just not right."

Sid took out my contract, looked at it for a while, then walked out of the room. About ten minutes later, he came back with a two-year contract that paid me $110,000 and $115,000.

He told me, "You're right. Here, sign it."

And I did. It was that simple. A month later, Sid resigned as head coach and Bud Adams named Bum Phillips as his replacement.

I liked Bum, but I really hadn't spent a lot of time with him and I hated the idea of playing for a defensive-minded coach. I called Bud Adams as soon as I heard the announcement.

"You're making a big mistake, Mr. Adams. Bum's a nice guy, but I really think King Hill should be the head coach."

Bud just blew me off, saying something about how Bum was the right man for the job and to give him a chance. But Bud didn't exactly have a great record with coaches. I had my doubts and the scars, broken bones and concussions to prove it. Bum was my fourth head coach in five seasons.

I didn't exactly trust Bud's word, either. My dad had a heart attack late in the season and I was anxious to see him. When I told Bud about it, he let me use his private plane to get to California and check on dad for a couple of days. I thought it was a great gesture on Bud's part and it turned out my dad would be fine. A few weeks later, I got a bill in the mail from Bud's office for $5,000 for leasing his plane. I thought, "thanks a lot, Bud." Nice gesture.

By the time the 1975 camp rolled around, two things convinced me Bum would be good for us and good for me. When I called King Hill to tell him I was sorry he didn't get a chance to become head coach, King told me, "Don't worry about it. You're going to like Bum. He's going to get it done."

That was a good enough endorsement for me, coming from the guy who, if he hadn't been around during those 1-13 years, I probably would have jumped off a building. And then Bum brought in a loud, gruff S.O.B. from San Diego that wasted no time telling me how the cabbage was going to be eaten from now on. Carl Mauck was a strong, no-nonsense, smart center that Bum brought in specifically to protect my ass. He and his wife, Vicki, invited me to dinner almost as soon as he got to town.

"We're going to work hard this off-season, Pastorini," Carl told me, "and you need to be here. You're the quarterback. You're gonna be here."

I told Mauck I had a few things I needed to get done, but, yeah, I'd be around.

"No. You're not going to be around. You're going to be here."

I knew immediately I had someone who was going to back me up. I also realized Bum knew the beating I took the previous four years. All the good teams were organizing their own off-season workouts as a group. Instead of running in a thousand different directions like cockroaches when the lights come on, after the season we all stayed around Houston for workouts. Carl was instrumental in getting everybody together. He was gruff, abrasive, grated on your nerves, used colorful language and pretty much growled at everybody. He called me a Wop. He told tasteless jokes. He called me and everyone on the team, every name in the book.

He spoke his mind publicly and privately. But he was a smart son of a bitch–a straight-A student at Southern Illinois–and that animal that was within him made him the perfect complement for me. I hated bullshitters. Carl was the same. I didn't know a damn thing about Carl before, but we became friends overnight and we all busted our asses that summer.

Bum changed the way we did business, too. He didn't make practices or workouts easier, but he did make them professional and made each player accountable not just for himself, but for others. At our first meeting, Bum announced, "We don't play the Houston Oilers this year. So we're not going to scrimmage the Houston Oilers. We're going to practice in helmets, shoulder pads and shorts. And the pads are just so you won't get hurt and get in some conditioning."

In other words, we didn't beat on each other. We ran hard, worked hard and practiced hard. Everything was done at a brisk pace. Even during training camp, we never spent more than an hour and forty-five minutes working out, from the time we hit the field until we were done. If I wanted to stay late and get in some extra throwing, fine. If guys wanted to get in some extra technique and practice time, great. But Bum had a laid-back approach and was approachable. He let players be themselves. He encouraged players to know each other.

After one of our first practices, Bum told me, "Dan, don't go out with Carl tonight. Go team up with Elvin and Curley and go do something together."

He did that often. He told all of us in meetings to go out with guys we normally didn't go out with. He ordered pizza and beer, brought it to the facility and told us to go sit with guys we didn't know. I did know everybody and hung out with everybody at some point or another, but I saw what was happening around me. We were jelling. We were trusting each other more than ever. I saw how Bum was building a team. Once the 1975 season began, on Thursday nights, Bum sent the entire team to the Swinging Door, a honky-tonk and barbecue joint in Richmond, near where Bum lived. When we got there, there would be pitchers of beer lined up for us, as much barbecue as we wanted, and tables for us to all sit down and share stories. Sometimes, Bum would invite us to his ranch in Richmond and we'd just hang out, drinking beer and bullshitting. There was a unique camaraderie building. People always talked about teams becoming families. Bum actually was turning us into a family. In the past, guys worked so hard at practices and got beat up so much during games, a lot of guys began resenting practices and being around one another. Bum made sure the exact opposite happened. It reminded me of my high school coach, John Hannah, who every once in a while invited some players to his house. His wife made a bunch of apple pies and would cut each player an entire quarter of a pie and heap it on a plate. It just made you feel like you were part of something, like you were king shit in the neighborhood.

For someone like me, always searching for the perfect family, always wanting to live up to expectations, that's what Bum's approach was doing for us. I would take a young receiver aside and show him some things I wanted him to do, and explained why I needed him to run a route a specific way. It was happening all over the locker-room. Carl gained the respect of the offensive line and was the unquestioned anchor. On the defensive side, Bum taught the 3-4 defense like a master, his son, Wade, was defensive line coach and guys like Curley Culp and Elvin Bethea mentored young talents like Robert Brazile, who was a ferocious pass-rusher.

Bum made a hell of a first-impression in 1975. We went 10-4. Unfortunately, that was only good enough for third-place in the toughest division in football and we missed the playoffs again. The highlight of the year for me came in Oakland, when we faced probably the best team in football at the time. My dad came to the game and it was a tough, see-saw battle with Ken Stabler and the Raiders. We were down 26-20 in the final minutes, when I took the team down the field and hit Mack Alston late with the game-winning touchdown pass. Mack had questionable hands on occasion, but he caught that one on his fingertips. When the game ended, dad rushed to the sideline and I told the usher, "He's my dad. He's with me."

He ran onto the field as time expired, I lifted him high into the air and told him, "We did it." What a great win.

Houston was falling in love with us. Bum was becoming a sensation, with his chewing tobacco, cowboy hat and the simple eloquent way he put things. He was pure country and pure Texas, but mostly pure football. And I was getting swept up in being the star quarterback. I got infatuated with it. I got drunk on it.

Houston was the Wild West and fit my free spirit perfectly. I was a California boy and not your basic kind of guy. I made a lot of headlines with the way I said exactly what I thought and brought some flair to a town that reflected the same things. Oil was booming. Watching football was cheap. A suite for 15 people at the Astrodome cost $5,000. I knew guys in my apartment complex, oil traders, that made that much money in a day.

The seats seven rows up behind our bench cost $7.50. You had roughnecks, guys that went straight out of high school to the oil fields or offshore rigs making more money in a month than they had their entire lives before that. It was the movie Giant. It was James Dean. It was Rock Hudson. It was audacious.

June and I went to a bar late in the year and as she stood there with her back to the bar, I faced her. Two girls sauntered up to us, one squeezed between June and me and said, "Do you screw as good as you play football?"

I stammered, craned my neck to look around her at June and said, "Uh . . . June?"

"Absolutely, he does," June told the girl, "even better."

June and I spent a lot of time apart and when she wasn't around, I threw myself into being the star quarterback and eventually threw away the best thing that had happened in my life. I was intoxicated with the attention around town. I had no conscience when it came to screwing around. I knew exactly what I was doing, but I was just consumed by it. It was insecurity, ego, that constant search for affirmation. I had June Wilkinson, for God's sakes. And I screwed it up. The relationship meant more to June than it did to me. All I ever wanted was to win and being with women was a sport to me, like everything else.

When I was with June, it was fantastic. I couldn't have been more excited about becoming a father. June had our baby girl in New Orleans, while June was on a promotional trip. We named our daughter Brahna because we saw a beautiful picture of a beautiful girl in a magazine, when June and I visited friends a few weeks earlier. The women in the magazine were dressed in Gone

With The Wind-style dresses. One of the models was named Brahna. I turned to June and said, "That's the name."

Eventually, June and I just weren't together very much. She enjoyed being in L.A. and my life was in Houston. Everybody thought I had it all, but emotionally I still wasn't equipped to be what June wanted. I didn't know what love was. To me, love was quantity not quality. Everything in my life was a material thing. Everywhere I went, there never was a problem finding a girl and it became a habit. It was a sport. It was an everyday deal: You got up, went to practice, went out, got drunk, found a girl and got laid. Then, you woke up the next morning to sweat it all out and do it all over again and make Happy Hour. I never had to work. Women in this town were just as loose and wild as the guys. I had eight years of Jesuit Catholic education, but it didn't stick. I had faith and I believed. But there were a lot of doctrines that I just didn't believe. I didn't know what I was looking for.

The only thing that grounded me was football. That's where I felt secure, because I knew the guys in that huddle would bust their asses for me and they knew I'd bust my ass for them. I never would cheat on those guys and I knew those guys in that huddle never would cheat on me. They never would steal from me like my brother-in-law. They never would ask me for something unless they really needed it. They wouldn't take advantage or try to change me like so many people had. Bum was becoming like a father to me. Carl was like my brother. I could tell those two guys things I never could tell any woman or even my family. My family crest was the oil derrick on the side of my helmet. I was living the life, but I was a lost soul.

CHAPTER EIGHT

Putting up walls

June knew I wasn't being faithful. I went to New York to visit a shoe sponsor and make a couple of appearances. I met a girl at a reception that I attended and wound up going back to her apartment. A couple hours later, the girl's phone rang. When she answered it, she turned to me with a strange look on her face and said, "It's for you."

I figured it was someone from the shoe company.

"Hello?"

I heard June's distinctive British voice, "You bahs-tard."

I had no idea how June knew I was there. I mean, this was a girl that I just met. June must have had me tailed. Somehow, though, June and I got through that. We both knew the end of our relationship was near and I even kidded June about what happened in New York, "I've got to admit, that was a great catch on your part."

As usual, I turned to my cynical sense of humor to deflect things. June wasn't amused. A few weeks later, while June was doing a show in Dallas, I went out, met another girl and went to her apartment. June wasn't supposed to come home until the next night. I spent the night at the girl's place, hung out with her all day and the next afternoon, I was fixing a couple of martinis at her place when there was a knock at the door. The girl opened the door just as I turned the corner with a couple of martinis. I saw June walk in, held out one martini, smiled and said, "You want one?

That was it. That was the end. There were no more chances with June. I blew it and it was an ugly divorce. June had a good attorney, who I actually knew. David Berg was a good guy, but you definitely wanted him on your side, not representing your pissed-off wife. We eventually settled everything, including child support, and I retreated back to within the shell of things that made me feel most secure and at home. Football, raising a little hell, picking up girls. And racing.

I met Jim Youngblood at a boat show in Houston. He owned Youngblood Boats. I marveled at one of his new jet boats at the show. Jim and I talked for a while and he knew I loved to drive.

"You want to race it?" he asked.

"I'd love to drive it if you're looking for a shoe," I told him.

I went to Memphis to test the boat. We decided to team together and race in the Southern Drag Boat Association. I won my first event at Lake Mizzel outside Liberty, Tx. just a few weeks later. I beat Porter McFarland in the final round, but only because Porter was a true sportsman. I was so nervous before the race, I couldn't get the motor started, because I forgot to turn on the fuel line. Porter was behind me on the lake, just circling, waiting. Other drivers wouldn't have done that. For most guys, if it's time to go and you're not ready, they go anyway, but Porter made a big circle behind me and when I finally got it started, we paired up and I went. In the previous race, my crew chief Bobby Rowe noticed that I let up a bit after I hit the throttle, so in the final he taped a rock to my foot, so I would remember not to lift it.

And it worked. I nailed the start, hammered the throttle and beat Porter. I wound up beating Porter a couple more times in races later in the year.

Eventually, I went back to Cabot, Ark. and helped Youngblood build and test a new boat that I called the Quarterback Sneak. I trailered it to California in my blazer and raced the next season in the National Drag Boat Association. That's where the big boys raced. It was a hell of a well-designed boat and it was fast. The operation was pretty small. I trailered the boat out to California, with a drum of Nitro and a toolbox in the back of my blazer. That was pretty much it. Gary McClendon, who built the boat with us, drove with me and we never stopped on the way to our first race, switching driving duties every few hours while the other guy slept. My sponsor was Larry Enderli, who loved racing, loved the Oilers and was from Baytown. Larry flew to California to meet us. When we picked up Larry at the airport, one of our competitors also standing by the luggage belt yelled, "Well, if it isn't the broken down ballplayer and hillbilly race team."

Larry looked over, kind of smiled and then lunged at the guy. We had to hold him back. Larry was just as competitive as the rest of us and from the start, our team clicked. In the first race of our first run at Lake Ming outside Bakersfield, we became the first jet boat ever to break the nine-second barrier in a race, running an 8.93. I lowered the record in a later run and then made the final. I took a lead in the championship race, but about halfway through the run, I kicked a rod out and the boat caught on fire. I had flames coming up through my crotch, all kinds of shit flying over my head and could barely see through my helmet, and still barely lost at the finish line. I figured I was done after that. I sure didn't want to invest in another motor, but I met Sid Waterman at that race and he sold me a couple of motors at a good price. We went to Phoenix the next week and lowered the world record yet again. We took the circuit by storm, eventually lowering the world record to 8.23 seconds. I set four world records in my first season in the NDBA.

In one of my last races before I had to start focusing on the 1976 season, I matched up with Porter yet again outside Starkville, Ms. As I sat in my boat getting ready to launch, Porter walked up to my boat and said, "Dan, I'm gonna beat you one of these days if it kills me."

I just froze. That's not something you say in racing, and Porter knew it. I just sat there, staring straight ahead. A weird feeling came over me. Gary looked at me and said, "You alright?"

"No. I don't feel right."

My forte in racing always was getting off the line first. From the time I raced midgets, to the dollar match races I ran in high school, I just never got beat off the line. It's what helped me compete against the best drivers even if I didn't have as much experience. But in that race, Porter beat me off the line, big-time. He put two boat lengths on me before I knew what happened. As I chased him down, all of a sudden I saw his boat tip upward and take off straight into the air like a rocket ship. As I jetted past him, it spun 180-degrees and when I looked back, I saw Porter flying off the boat and tumble into the lake. I coasted through the finish line and then motioned for the pickup boat to come get me. I hopped on the pick-up boat and ran toward Porter, who was floating awkwardly in the water. I tried to reach down with a couple of other guys on the crew to pick up Porter, but it was like trying to pick up a bag of rocks. His body was just broken in half. He was a hard racer. He was a great guy. He was dead before we even got to him.

I didn't talk to very many people about that race. I did that ostrich thing again, just burying my head in the sand. I set it aside and focused on the upcoming season. I put up a wall. There were high hopes all over town, but we couldn't even do wrong right in 1976. It was just one of those things when young players are coming in and older players are headed out, plus we had a lot of injuries. We went 5-9, losing four games by less than a touchdown. I wasn't happy, because I thought we'd make the playoffs, but I trusted Bum and there wasn't any question he was the right guy that could get us to the post-season. At Baltimore midway through a six-game losing streak in the middle of the year, we were getting drilled. I had memories of the games in '71 and '72 when I saw guys quit. I wasn't going to let that happen again. I came to the sideline after a bad series, kicked a water jug, knocked stacks of cups off a table and pushed over a Gatorade bucket. Bum turned toward me and motioned for me to come see him.

I thought, "Ah, shit."

"Dan, I think you need to take a seat for a while."

"I'm sorry, Bum, I'll be alright."

"No. You need to sit."

Bum took charge and I liked that. I didn't like getting benched, but I knew it was my own fault and Bum handled it like a pro. He didn't show me up, or yell and scream. He just told me how things were going to be. I could tell Bum saw things in me that could help us win, but he also knew he needed to keep me in check sometimes.

I spent the next off-season drag boat racing again. Why not? It was in my blood, I loved it and I needed to get away, with my divorce from June being finalized. We were having another big year, winning races and drawing a lot of fans to events. Race promoters loved having the popular, so-called unpredictable quarterback racing.

In May, we went back to Lake Mizzel in Liberty and I was feeling pretty good. We had a great boat. It was a great-running boat and a straight-running boat, the only hitch being the occasionally difficult shut-down. When the Quarterback Sneak stopped, it stopped fast. My boat went close to 140-mph on the water and when I would hit top speeds, the only thing in the water would be the intake. Everything else was out of the water, pitching back and forth. We called it pig-walking and it's what made drag-boat racing so great for fans, the boat rocking back-and-forth, sort of shimmying and only the back-edge of the boat actually in the water. I lined up for my first race and there was a great crowd on the shore watching. I quickly became one of the more popular racers on the drag-boat circuit and Lake Mizzel wasn't far from Houston, so a lot of Oilers fans were there, too. There were ropes along the shore to control the crowd and it was packed.

When I hit the throttle I did what I always did. I jumped to a quick lead and flew toward the finish line. As I crossed the finish line, I let off the motor and the left edge of my tri-hull boat tipped into the water. My boat immediately, uncontrollably veered 90-degrees to the left, toward the shore, as it was going about 130-mph. The force slammed me under the deck and when I fell, I hit the throttle with my ribs. The kill switch for the motor was clipped to the back of my life vest and didn't pull out, but when I fell on the throttle, it didn't matter. The boat hit the shore and launched into the air. I was pinned under the deck, looking toward the sky, hearing thuds and bumps, then all of a sudden flying through the air. I knew the boat eventually would hit something and I just thought, "I'm going to die."

I was in the air for what felt like forever. I saw the tops of trees and branches flying by. I probably was 30-feet high. Then, I felt a thud and all kinds of scratching and rolling. The boat slid into the parking lot on its side, between two motor homes sideways, then flattened out and came to rest against a Toyota Corolla. I was rattled, but tried to compose myself and climb out of the boat. I was still in the boat when I saw Gary McClendon running toward me.

"How bad is it?" I asked him.

"Bad," he said. "Really bad."

There was a man at the finish line that had an instamatic camera. He walked under the restraining rope into the water, because he wanted a shot of me coming through the finish line. When my boat veered toward the shore, I hit him with the hull of my boat and just about sliced him in half. His name was Dale Johnson. He was 33-years-old, a husband and a father. There was another girl, a 10-year-old named Sherry Gaskins, who was hit in the side of the head by the nozzle of my boat as it launched into the air. She died, too.

When I got to the shoreline and saw what happened, I fell to my knees and lost it. I wept and wept some more. My entire body shook. I was devastated, shocked, scared. There was just nothing I could do. The entire scene was surreal, officers and county deputies everywhere, folks staring at the victims, sirens blaring, ambulances driving up. Eventually it was determined my boat flew more than 100-feet through and over the crowd.

It didn't take long for the rumors and whispers to start. Was Pastorini drinking? Was he out of control? Was he reckless? None of it was true. I certainly was no angel. But when it came to racing, there was no messing around. There never was any drinking or any cutting corners in my pits. After the races? Yes. But when we were in the pits working on machines, we never messed around. It didn't take long for the lawsuits to come, too.

I held fundraisers for the families. I sold my house to pay off the settlements for the families. I went to the funerals. I tried to talk with the families. But I felt totally helpless and nothing I did felt like enough. One family lost their husband and father. Another family lost their child. And I was responsible for both. It was the worst feeling in my life and I knew no matter how long I lived, part of me never would get over it. For weeks after the accident, when I went to bed at night I could smell the nitro fumes from that day. Sometimes, I closed my eyes and saw the dead branches flying over me, against the blue sky. I kept telling myself, move on, move on, move on. My teammates were supportive. They knew it was an accident and a lot of guys kicked in donations for the families and were very supportive of the families. Three drivers on the drag-boat circuit died in races that summer. I should have died in Liberty. I was being drained of money and my emotions were strained.

Still, it didn't take long for me to start acting like my same, old self. Maybe I was just that self-centered. Maybe I was an unfeeling egomaniac. Maybe I just put myself in survival mode. But as cold-hearted as it was, by the end of the summer I convinced myself that the divorce and the accident were behind me. I believed I had 50 other families depending on me. Or, maybe I just put up another wall.

CHAPTER NINE

A small Armenian family . . . and Black Mollies

A few weeks before training camp in 1977, Don Meredith put together a quarterback legends charity golf tournament in Hawaii. It was a great event and a good time for me to get away. Some of the greatest quarterbacks in NFL history were invited, as well as quarterbacks of my era like Roger Staubach and Tommy Kramer. Bobby Layne was there. Billy Kilmer. Johnny Unitas. Sonny Jurgenson. It was a posh event, sponsored by a hotel chain and supported by huge corporate sponsors. Bobby Layne was social chairman, so it basically was three days of golf, booze and stories.

Tommy Kramer and I were playing catch on the grass in front of the hotel before cocktail hour one evening, when Billy Kilmer started hollering at me from the balcony of his fourth-floor room. Apparently he was bragging about my arm strength to Bobby Layne, Johnny Unitas and sportswriter Dan Jenkins, all of whom were sitting on the balcony with Kilmer having cocktails, solving the world's problems and talking about quarterbacks.

"Throw the ball up here," Kilmer shouted. "Hit me, Dante. Can you hit me?"

Naturally, I wasn't going to let a chance to show off pass me by. I cocked my arm and threw a perfect spiral as hard as I could. The ball sailed perfectly over their heads, above the balcony, above the next floor and hit a 10th-story balcony.

Jenkins turned to Bobby Layne and said, "Did you see that? Can you believe the arm strength in that kid? Can you believe he threw a football up 10-stories?"

Unitas chimed in, "Yeah, but his receiver was on the fifth floor."

I laughed when I heard what Unitas said, but those were the kinds of comments that grated on me. That's how my career was defined. He's got a great arm, but . . .

Another quarterback legend, John Hadl, helped me a lot in 1977. He was a 14-year veteran that had seen it all. He convinced me to just keep working like I was working and keep playing hard. Hadl and I got along great, too, because he really knew football and liked having a good time off the field.

About three-weeks into training camp in Nacogdoches, Tx., Hadl and I had about enough of our new offensive coordinator Ken Shipp's meetings. We knew the offense better than he did. I'd called my own plays for going on seven years and worked my ass off in camp. We were at a bar after practice for a while, when Hadl and I started throwing back peppermint Schnapps. Mauck stood up when we were about four schnapps in, about 5:30, and said, "OK, time for the meeting."

"We ain't going," I said.

Mauck argued with us for a while, but he knew Hadl and I weren't going and we'd had our fill of Shipp. It was easy to get frustrated with Shipp. He was an Xs and Os guy who thought he knew everything there was to know about football because he watched tape back and forth, in slow-motion, forward and backwards until his eyes bled. Shipp was fine on the chalk board or scribbling on a piece of paper. The problem was Shipp didn't really know shit when it came to actually playing the game full-speed. I always studied hard. I always watched film. I always enjoyed the chess game that was a part of football. But I learned the most on the field, when bullets were flying, because that's how you learn to make adjustments and reads in a split second. Hadl had 14-years in the league. Shipp held a meeting just for the sake of holding a meeting, so Hadl and I decided to pass.

We didn't know Bum was going to gather the entire team together and tell the team just how proud he was of the hard work we'd put in for three-weeks under steamy Texas conditions.

"I want to congratulate everybody," Bum told the team. "It's been long and hot and you all have done a great job. Everyone's worked hard. Everyone's been committed. No one's been late to any practices or meetings . . .

That's when Mauck shouted at Bum.

"Oh, yeah? What about your quarterbacks?"

Bum looked around the room.

"Dan? John? . . . Pastorini? Hadl?"

John and I were in no shape to leave the bar. It was one of those nights. We both felt like cutting loose and we did. Around 11 p.m., we decided we should get back to our dorms and make amends with our teammates. I pulled into Jack In The Box to order about 50 hamburgers for the guys. As I tried to order the food, stumbling and stammering as I shouted at the Jack clown, Hadl got sick in my new truck. He literally was falling down drunk. I kicked open his door and he started puking on the ground, as I held him by the back of his shirt. He kept puking, until I pulled up my truck to the drive-thru window and he fell out the door into a thick blackberry bush that was about four-feet high, and a puddle of his own puke. I ran around the truck, pulled him out of the bush and dragged Hadl into the bed of my truck, because he smelled so bad. He had cuts on his arms and neck, scratches all over his face and was dripping with puke and beer. I picked up the bags of hamburgers, grabbed one and stuck it out the window in John's face as I drove off back to camp, just to be a smartass.

"Want a cheeseburger, John?"

He groaned and rolled over in the bed of the truck. When we got back to the dorm, it only got worse. The vets were hazing the rookies with fire extinguishers, spraying powder everywhere. Hadl turned purple. At breakfast the next morning, Hadl and I had Schnapps hangovers, which are the worst, and we sat side-by-side, just completely raw. Bum sat down in front of us.

"What in the hell were you two doing?"

It was as if we rehearsed our reply, but we didn't. Simultaneously, Hadl and I told Bum, "Coach, it seemed like the right thing to do at the time."

Bum laughed and said, "You know I gotta fine you."

"Yeah, put it on the tab," I said.

The friction with Shipp got to be pretty deep-ceded. Before warm-ups every day we did these scrimmage plays called take-offs. The first-team offense, then the second-team offense, jogged through some simple plays. It was easy stuff, just to get the blood going and get warmed up.

When Hadl stepped up to the line after our long night out, Shipp called out a play neither of us knew and said, "OK, run it!"

"What is that?" John told him.

"Well, if you would have been at the meeting last night you'd know what it was."

I was about to step in and tell Shipp what he could do with his damn meeting, but Hadl handled it. Here was John Hadl, 14-years in the league, one of the best quarterbacks in history, old No. 21. And this asshole was trying to treat him like a middle-schooler?

"Hey, mother fucker," Hadl told Shipp, "just tell me the play and I'll run it."

Shipp mumbled something and then gave Hadl another play to run.

On top of the fine Bum gave us, John and I had to run a mile after practice and we spent it just laughing our asses off about the night before, imitating Shipp and laughing at his dumb ass.

It was just an ongoing thing between Shipp and me, just growing tension and frustration. He just had this power trip thing going, like he had to show me how much football he knew. We started the season hot, winning three of our first four games, but things began unraveling after that. We were just a team that needed to come together and needed a jolt of good luck. Except for Robert Brazile, most of our draft picks in '75 and '76 didn't work out. We traded away a kid I thought would be pretty good–Steve Largent. And John Matuszak, who we took No. 1 overall in '73, didn't work out with us, went AWOL and wound up in the World Football League, before latching on with the Raiders. Bum was putting his stamp on the team with hard-working guys that maybe didn't grab a lot of headlines or look pretty, but got the job done. He said, "I want players that work like country kids work. Get up early and just get the job done."

I liked the way we had guys who were hungry and weren't trying to impress anyone. We had guys that just wanted to play. We picked up late-round picks and free agents that just bought into what Bum was selling—Rob Carpenter, Mo Towns, Tim Wilson, Ken Kennard, George Reihner, Mike Reinfeldt. The epitome of them all was our kicker, Toni Fritsch. He was a frumpy, short, Austrian with a spare tire, a thick mustache and wore football pants that were two sizes too big. But man, could he kick.

Toni walked onto the practice field one day, Bum looked at him, shook his head and said, "Toni, you look like you've got a small Armenian family living in those pants."

Toni made everybody laugh and took pride in making clutch kicks. I was his holder.

"I have ice-water in my veins," Toni told me.

At Green Bay the second week of the season, the field-goal team rushed out late in the half to kick a field goal and Toni was nervous as hell, pulling on his pants, fidgeting, trying to rush to get lined up. As I took a knee and started counting players to make sure we were set, his eyes were the size of saucers and he told me in his accent, "Hurry, Dante, hurry, Dante."

Right before I took the snap, I turned and looked at him.

"How's that ice-water working out, Toni?"

We were close to turning the corner. We beat the Steelers in the 'Dome to go 3-1, then things started unraveling. Shipp took it upon himself to figure out that my reads and checks were the problem.

During a midseason slump, Shipp was clicking and clicking the remote as we watched tape in a meeting room. He kept telling me what I should have been looking for from every guy on the opposing defense on every snap. It took him an hour and a half to run through 15 plays.

"You should have read the cornerback's right foot," he told me.

"You should have seen the defensive ends line up six-inches further outside," he said.

It was just meaningless bullshit, on and on. Finally, I just reached over, grabbed the clicker out of his hand and threw it.

"Give me that damn thing," I told him.

I started the video and rattled off everything I saw in real time, as the film was moving, without stopping the tape once.

I told Shipp, "Now tell me what they're doing. Now tell me what the keys are. You can't, can you?"

"You know what I see? I see the strong safety up, so I'm looking for a three-sky here. OK, now the safeties are deep, I'm looking for either a weak rotation or a double zone here."

Sure enough, everything that I said would happen, happened on both plays. I ran through the whole damn film without stopping it once. I got most of the reads perfect. I called every check, perfect.

"I don't need your goddamn, 'Well, when his feet are like this, you need to look for that.' Screw that, Ken. That's not how it works. I don't need to hear, 'When he's leaning this way, or looking over here, do this' I don't need that shit."

I snapped my fingers.

"I have this much time to react and you're wasting my time with this little meaningless bullshit."

I walked out of the room. It was a bad year, not anything like what we expected. When we finished 8-6, I convinced myself that my divorce and the accidents hadn't weighed on my mind. Usually, I'm always able to set things aside and focus on the games, but they probably were a distraction at some level.

I got beat up pretty good all year. I broke a couple of ribs, got my bell rung a few times and my collarbone and shoulder constantly were sore. That game we won against Pittsburgh was the most physical game any of us had ever played in. They were the team to beat and we got into an absolute war with them. I got carried off the field, Hadl got hurt and by the end of the game Guido Merkens, a utility guy and receiver, was taking snaps. The next day there were 23 players on the injured list between the two teams. I'd never seen a game when both teams were down to their third-string quarterbacks. Terry Bradshaw got hurt, Mike Kruczek got hurt and Tony Dungy was taking snaps for them. It was a bloodbath.

They returned the favor in another physical game in Pittsburgh and we just kept sliding after that. We didn't make the playoffs, but after '77 the Steelers knew and we knew that we would be their toughest opponent from that point on. The one thing Bum established once and for all in '77 was a roster of guys that wouldn't back down from any fight, anywhere. We were as close-knit a team as I'd ever been a part of. Sure, the way we played was taking its toll on all of us, but everyone was hungry and everyone was hurt. We didn't care what we had to do, we were going to be there for our teammates every Sunday unless we literally could not stand up.

I started relying heavily on pills to keep me going. I didn't even know what they were, but they kept us on the roster and they kept us able to function off the field, too. I took mostly Desoxyn, Red-and-Yellows and Black Mollies. I took Desoxyn for hangovers. I took handfuls of Red-and-Yellows for pain, sometimes two or three times over the course of a game. I took Desoxyn to get energized. I started thinking I could control how I felt pretty easily. If I felt shitty, I took a pill to make myself feel better. If I felt real good, I took a pill to mess myself up. It's like I was chemically controlled.

I mean, when I was a rookie one of my linemen, Bob Young, talked about taking steroids. I was sure a lot of guys were taking steroids by '77, just like a lot of guys couldn't function without pain pills. But nobody asked and nobody cared, least of all me. Those guys were protecting my ass, you think I'm going to care? You think anyone cared? None of it was under doctor's supervision. Some guys were taking drugs to a level where no man should go. It's how you survived.

On off days, we went just as hard. Sometimes we had Mondays off, sometimes we had Tuesdays. My biggest party night was Thursday. I could raise hell on Thursdays, then be done until after the game on Sunday. We'd hit Happy Hour, get a little buzz going and then start looking for girls. I always had the attitude of, I'm just going to be myself. I couldn't be a phony, for better or worse. Bum didn't care what you were or where you were from, so long as you played. If you did what you were told, showed up and played hard, he didn't care. He didn't care if you had long hair. He didn't care if you were black or white. He just wanted you to do your job. Sometimes, Bum gave me a couple-hundred bucks and said, "Take the guys out and make sure everybody has a good time."

It was a camaraderie thing and I was social chairman. We rented a place over by the Savannah Club near town and we had a room where we'd have barbecue, pizza and a bunch of beer. We'd drink for a couple of hours, hang out, then go our separate ways. We owned whatever club and disco we walked into, places like Daddy's Money, Friday's, Caligula's, Sam's Boat, Vic Taylor's Namedropper Club, Gilley's, whatever. The Oilers were becoming the biggest thing in town.

When I walked into a club, I always felt the eyes on me. It's the same thing I felt when I first walked into the cafeteria at Santa Clara. I was the blue-chipper. I was the guy that was supposed to save the Oilers and I had yet to live up to that tag. Fans respected the way I played, but whenever we fell short like in '77, it was open season on me.

By the time the season ended, all the papers and reporters picked apart my game. They said I was under-achieving. They wondered if I had what it took. Nothing hurt more than people calling me a loser or saying I should be traded. I had my car vandalized again after a game. I had played seven years in the NFL, but not once in a playoff game. I heard so many people blaming me, I started thinking maybe it was me. When I went home at the end of the season, I decided that if we didn't make the playoffs in 1978, things might need to change.

CHAPTER TEN

"I think I need the day off."

I finally got offered the big contract I'd been wanting before the 1978 season, and I knew that so long as I structured it right I could be set up for life. It was a simple negotiation. Bum, me, my agent Tommy Vance and Pat Peppler, the assistant general manager, went to dinner. We were determined to get the contract done in one night and to do it in a civil manner. Bum and Peppler finally hit the number that we wanted, but Pepplar asked, "Would you take deferred compensation?"

I actually was hoping for deferred compensation. We convinced them to bump the number a little, since I would take deferred compensation, and then I could spread the salary over several years and not have to worry about falling into another financial mess like I did with my brother-in-law Stan. The contract was a six-year deal and the highest in the NFL, worth $2.1 million. I would earn $150,000 a year, with another $200,000 deferred over 20-years, beginning in 1985. I protected myself. I knew I was getting toward the end of my career, my body had taken a beating and I was thinking about my retirement security. The first three years of the contract were guaranteed when I signed it. The second three years would be guaranteed when I passed a physical before the 1981 season.

That's all I had to do. Just pass the physical. It was a fair deal. It was fair for them and fair for me.

When I signed the deal, I told Bum that I was thinking about getting into drag-racing. He told me flat-out, no. Bum never told guys how to live their lives off the field. He used to tell us, "You know what's at stake." He told reporters the only off-season activity he discouraged was, "rattlesnake hunting."

Bum put it in my contract that I could no longer race boats or cars. After the accident at Lake Mizzel, I started watching and traveling to more car events and was hooked. Racing just ran through my veins, I wanted it so badly. I built a relationship with Raymond Beadle, a huge star in Funny Car racing and he told me I could excel as a Top Fuel dragster driver. He wanted us to be a team—he would drive the Blue Max Funny Car and I would drive the Blue Max Top Fuel car, but that dream would have to wait.

I was in California when I heard we traded Jimmie Giles for Earl Campbell out of Texas. I didn't understand why we would trade three picks and one of my tight ends, Jimmie Giles, for Earl. I heard of Earl, but we had a couple of good running backs in Ron Coleman and Rob Carpenter and Heisman Trophies didn't mean anything to me. Just because you won the Heisman Trophy doesn't mean you're the best football player out there. Jimmie was kind of a strange guy, a different breed of cat, kind of a smartass, but he was a hell of a talent and I thought we needed that kind of weapon. I thought we would have a real shot in '78 because of all the ingredients. We needed maybe a little help in the offensive line and maybe a wide receiver, but I certainly didn't think we needed a running back. To trade a proven tight end like Giles for an unproven running back, I didn't buy into it all the way. I felt a little different after I spoke with John Hadl. He had a friend on the University of Texas coaching staff that said this Campbell kid was an unbelievable talent.

"Yeah? Well I guess we'll see."

I showed up at training camp in San Angelo in my Chevy truck, with a low-rider Harley Davidson tied down in the bed and towing a Glastron ski boat. We probably were the only team that looked forward to going to training camp. In a lot of ways, it was more like a vacation. We worked hard, but Bum made it fun.

Bum just shook his head when he saw me roll up, honking and waving at him, with a big smile on my face, pulling my motorcycle and boat. I told Bum I needed to ski to work on my arm strength and I wasn't leaving camp until I gave him a ride on my Harley.

"You will never, ever get me on that thing," Bum said.

"It's just like riding one of your horses, Bum, only faster."

Before camp even started, I took one of our trainers skiing and he fell and broke his ankle.

"No more skiing," Bum told me. "Burn the skis."

Camp still was fun. I did a lot of boating, worked hard, rode my Harley. I did some homework on Earl to see what kind of player and person he was and kept hearing nothing but great things. I read a lot about him and admired the relationship he had with his momma. When I saw him at training camp, I walked up to Earl and said, "I like the way you talk about your mother. That's impressive. Welcome to the team."

Earl was impressive-looking. He was low to the ground, moved well and was faster than I thought he would be. He looked like a bulldozer, but I couldn't believe his speed. There was a lot of hype about Earl and what his addition would do for our team. I started thinking about the play-action pass plays I would call and all the ways we would use Earl.

Training camp actually was fun, with a lot of energy and anticipation. After practice, we would head to a bar together or Fisher Lake, to jet around on my boat. Because of Bum, we were all confident. We had something started. We had a camaraderie that I'd never seen before, meshed together and played as a team. Bum never said a word about us going to bars and the lake. He realized the boat was just another tool for us to bond and get closer. He was a smart man and someone every player on the team loved. Everyone in that locker-room respected the hell out of Bum.

The second night of training camp, I was running late for our 7 p.m. meeting, which was in an auditorium on the opposite side of campus. It was less than five-minutes until seven, so I hopped on my Harley and started tearing away. I looked to my right and saw Bum jogging out of the building next to my dorm. He was late for his own meeting.

I laughed and told Bum, "You can make it if you hop on my bike."

"Ah, shit," he said.

I zipped across campus, making as many sharp turns as I could, as Bum held on to the back of the bike with one hand and held his hat with the other.

It didn't take long to figure out Earl might become the most dominating rusher the league had seen since Jim Brown. The only things were, he wasn't Walter Payton. He wasn't elusive, so he had to be patient for holes to open. This wasn't college anymore, where Earl was just better than everybody and there were gaping holes. And Earl definitely wasn't a receiver. He just didn't have very good hands. So we kept it simple. Timmy Wilson was the truck and Earl was the trailer. In our first couple of preseason games, Earl had a hard time adjusting to the pro game. He kept running into the backs of our offensive linemen, to the point Carl came back to the huddle a couple times, screaming, "Goddammit, open your eyes." Guys on the offensive line constantly told him, "Patience, rook." Our line helped Earl a lot, although we suffered a setback when Greg Sampson got hurt during a drill, getting accidentally kicked in the head. Doctors eventually found a blood clot on Greg's brain and he underwent surgery. I told Bum that if I had to take a pay cut to make sure Greg got paid, I'd do it. I didn't want Greg to have to worry about getting cut in the middle of all the other things he was going through.

One of our preseason games was at Philadelphia and it was the first time I saw Sid Gilman since he left. When he left, I thought to myself, good frickin riddance, but he taught me a lot of football. Before the game, I walked straight up to him.

"You know what, coach?"

"What's that?"

"You were an asshole, but you taught me a lot of football."

"You know what? I was. And I apologize for that. If I didn't think you were the most talented guy I'd been around, I wouldn't have been such an ass."

When we finally got Earl to wait for the hole, it was electric. Earl never disappointed and he definitely put asses in seats. Everyone wanted to see the Tyler Rose now that he was a pro. The thing that bothered me was his slowness getting up and back to the huddle. He didn't understand the play clock and how much it drove me nuts, because I'm calling plays out there. I finally just started going to the line and called plays. Bum wanted to run Earl 20 or 25 times a game and keep a balance with the play-action pass and put Earl in one-on-one situations. In our season-opening game at Atlanta, it worked perfectly, when I pump-faked one way and hit earl on a little screen that he took 73-yards for a touchdown. When I got to the bench, I found out they called it a running play, even though it was a pass. That put 73-yards on Earl's rushing total and took 73-yards off my passing total. I thought, "Oh, that's how it's going to be."

We lost the opener to Atlanta and I got crushed a couple of times. On the second sack, I cracked a rib on my left side and there was some internal bleeding. I also separated my throwing shoulder. I was hospitalized and listed as doubtful for our second game at Kansas City, but I knew there was no way I wasn't going to play. After all the shit I'd been through, all the criticism, all the injuries and never missing games, I wasn't going to miss this ride no matter what happened. We fell behind 17-6 against the Chiefs, but we had a couple of fourth-quarter touchdown drives to win it on the road.

I was hurting, but felt damn good about the season, with Earl looking so good. But I still didn't think Ken Shipp was the guy to help our offense reach its potential. We shouldn't have lost the opener and our other two wins were more difficult than they needed to be. I didn't want to get Earl killed out there and I knew the only way we could get through teams like Pittsburgh was with a balanced attack.

Against the Rams in the fourth game of the season, we trailed late and Shipp got desperate. I'd been calling plays and we were on the 40-yard line moving the ball. He sent in a deep-go route and I didn't want to run it because their safeties were playing deep, but I did. The route was double-covered, of course. Pat Thomas intercepted the ball and I got booed off the field. I was so pissed off, because we had field-position, Earl was pounding them, caving in Isaiah Robertson's chest on one play, and we had openings underneath. Why the hell Shipp called that go was beyond me. What the hell did he see? It was another game we should have won.

The next morning I picked up the paper and the headline said, "Shipp: 'I don't know why Pastorini called that play'"

What the hell? He blamed me? I already was getting criticism for my play-calling and now he put the loss on me. I was at the facility by 6:30, waiting for his ass. He walked in smoking a pipe, "Hey, Pasto," and went into his office.

I wanted the entire team to hear what I had to tell him, because I was the leader. I didn't want them to start doubting my play-calling. So I shouted his name across the room to get his attention and when he turned around I laid into him.

"Alright, mother fucker, you cast the first stone. You don't ever sell me out like that when it was your dumb ass that blew that call. You think you can get away with that? When this is done, we'll see who is left standing."

Bum called a team meeting, but I stayed at my locker, staring at the floor. I thought about just apologizing and moving on, but I couldn't. I decided I was going to stick to my convictions even if it cost me my job. I knew we could be a great team. I knew we were good enough to get to the Super Bowl, but we weren't going to win with this incompetent guy running the offense. He was a shitty coach and I wasn't going to act like he wasn't, even if it meant that they would play my backup Gifford Nielsen.

Bum came to my locker and said, "Come on, Dan, let's go to the meeting."

I said, "Bum, I think you either need to get rid of him or play Gifford. I can't play for him anymore. And I think I need the day off, Bum."

I walked out as Bum yelled at me, "Dan! Dan!"

I turned around at the doorway and said, "Do what you gotta do, boss."

I didn't want to go to my apartment, because I knew they'd come looking for me, or send my neighbor Barry Warner after me. Barry was a local radio guy that covered the team. Anytime I was out too late or they couldn't find me, they sent Barry after me. So I drove to Beaumont to spend the day dove hunting with my agent Tommy Vance. As I drove down Interstate-10, I turned on the radio and every station was talking about me "storming out of practice." I mean, every station had some sort of comment about me leaving the facility, how there was dissension and was I going to be cut from the team.

"Nobody's seen Pastorini," one guy said. "He's whereabouts unknown. If you see him, call the station."

Tommy invited the Game Warden, Beaumont's Chief of Police and a county sheriff hunting. As I sat outside Beaumont drinking beer with the guys after the hunt, Tommy turned on a radio.

The timing was amazing. Just as Tommy turned on the radio, the DJ said, "Does anyone know where Pastorini is?"

The Sheriff raised his hand, "I do!"

When I got home around 9 p.m., I saw Bum and Carl in my driveway, sitting in Bum's truck.

I told Bum, "This guy's a cancer. He's going to ruin our team. He can't coach a lick. Why don't you put King Hill in charge?"

"That's what I'm going to do."

The next day, Bum told Shipp, "I need my starting quarterback more than I need you as offensive coordinator."

That's the day we became a dominant team. I was confident again and confident in King Hill. Our defense was terrorizing people. The offense was getting better every week, with Earl running all over. It didn't matter who we played, where we played or if we fell behind. We could beat anybody. We won at Cleveland. We were down 23-points at New England and came back to win when I started running more play-action to keep them off of Earl. The Steelers were 7-0 to start the year and we went to Pittsburgh and beat them for our first Monday Night win. Earl scored three touchdowns and I hit 13-of-19 passes and wasn't sacked. After the game, I sat at my locker lost in the moment of where I had been and where I was now. My face must have been glazed over, looking off into the distance because Gifford tapped me on the shoulder and said, "Dan, where are you?"

I wasn't that much older than Giff, but I looked at him like a father would look at a son and told him, "Giff, you don't know what has happened here in eight years. I've survived all of it. I hope you never have to go through it. And you know, right now, it was all worth it, just so I could be here with these guys tonight. This is my family."

I called every play at the line of scrimmage and could audible out of any play, to any play. I played mind-games with the defenses we faced. I had calls to go from a run to a pass, from a pass to a run, or any pass in the playbook to any other pass in the playbook. I would walk up to the line, look at what we were facing and it became easy picking people apart.

I'd tell myself, OK, I got Ace formation, where are you going to put your strong safety? Wherever you put him, I'm attacking your weak side. I'm going to throw that way or run that way. It took some learning on each of our player's part, but when we got it, God, it was such an easy and beautiful thing. There always was a good call. We might have gotten beat on some plays, but it was because they beat us. I could look at the front, look at the linebacker force, what the safeties were doing, and I had a whole menu of plays I could run. It was clockwork. If I wanted short motion, I showed my receivers the heel of my right foot. If I wanted whole motion to flip the strength of the field, I showed the whole leg. We had supreme confidence and I was having the most fun I'd ever had playing football. We were winning and everyone loved the Oilers. Earl was a hero, Bum was a down-home icon and I was the so-called untamed playboy quarterback. When we walked into bars, there would be pitchers of beer standing in a line, waiting for us. We had girls, money and we couldn't be beat. We owned the city.

A promotional picture my senior year at Santa Clara.

*Am I young or what This was taken right after I gave up
a baby for adoption.*

At the airport in Houston, coming back from the 1979
AFC Championship Game. Bum and I were the only
ones who knew I'd played my last game for the Oilers.

Blowing into my breathalyzer. I had to do it everyday,
twice a day, for more than a year.

Cathy Lyons on the left, Pam, Meemaw and Keith Lyons.
That's my family.

*Chicago All Star game against the Super Bowl champion
Colts. I kicked, punted and quarterbacked*

*Getting carted off the field with two ribs completely
broken and another fractured.*

*Huge crowd at Pomona. They're hanging off the rails
-- they love Top Fuel, man.*

I bought a '76 Porsche on eBay and this was the ultimate machine we built out of it. It was 386-horsepower, air-cooled motor. This was the car that got me back into road racing.

*In a storm in New England. That's my old roomate,
George Webster, coming after me.*

*Jim Plunkett and me, a couple of California boys at the
Chicago All Star Game.*

*Just trying to do what I could do to help Jim Plunkett
and Tom Flores, the week after I came back from surgery.*

Me and L.C. Greenwood at another get-together at Three Rivers.

Me and my buddy Carl on a little Sunday afternoon stroll.

Mixing nitro for the next race.

My daughter, Brahna. That's every father's nightmare
-- a daughter that likes all the same toys you like.

My favorite picture of Brahna and June.

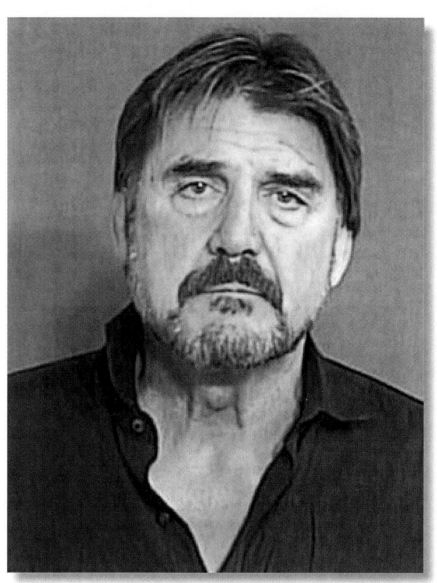

My mugshot. The lowest point.

My rookie year with the Oilers. Those were our Oilers practice jerseys. I had no idea everything I would go through.

Promo picture for the Silver Bullet . . .
it's Pam's favorite picture of me.

Signing autographs at a race. Man, we had a great fan base.

Signing my letter-of-intent to go to Santa Clara. It actually was a baseball scholarship, but that's my football coach, Pat Malley.

*Swig Hall, where I threw a baseball from the courtyard in
front of the building to the street on the other side. Kids at
Santa Clara have been trying to do it ever since. No one has.*

*That's Jim Brissette on the right, as I take the tool tray off
the motor, getting ready to crank it up.*

The catch that never was. Mike Renfro pulls in the touchdown that should have changed the AFC title game. Today, this play wouldn't even be reviewed.

The coldest game I ever played, in Cleveland. Parts of the tarp were frozen on the field. You couldn't penetrate the ground with your cleats, so we wore tennis shoes.

The last game I played for the Raiders. I'm convinced Al Davis didn't want me around because he was afraid Plunkett would crumble.

The life of a quarterback.

There's my buddy, Diron Talbert, and Conway Hayman
in front . . . Hey, what are you looking at, Conway

This was Luv Ya Blue, man. It was Camelot.

CHAPTER ELEVEN

The Bandage Bowl

We had a wild group of guys. In any other environment, we couldn't have all gotten along the way we did. I could walk into that locker-room anytime I wanted and when I looked around the room, I could point to a racist, a religious fanatic, a thief, a deviant and just about every other kind of character imaginable. But once we were together we were a special team. That's what made us the Oilers. Everyone wanted to be around us and we enjoyed being around everyone.

Our post-game hangout was Vic Taylor's Name-Dropper Club. One of the girls I dated during the season was named Marcia and Marcia didn't like that there were other girls I dated. I had several beers when Marcia came into the Name-Dropper Club and started yelling at me. Of course, I yelled back and we took it outside, screaming at each other. She called me a few choice names, then slammed her car door shut and tore off toward the front of the club and the street. Mauck and some of the guys were giving me a hard time about getting told off, so I thought, screw it. If you want to end this, let's end it in style. I took my beer mug, grabbed it like a football and hurled it at her car as she sped off. The mug probably went 60-yards in the air, over some power line and crashed into the back window of her car, shattering the glass. It was a great throw.

When I turned back toward Carl and the guys, he told me, "That's the best throw you've ever made."

Whenever we walked into a bar or a party, we made sure we had a good time. I went to a party that was supposed to be a nice birthday celebration for a friend, but wound up smoking some pot and jumping in the pool with two girls who wanted to have some fun. The pool had a stone archway bridge over the middle. Someone ordered a Mariachi group to play for the party, so the Mariachis stood on the bridge watching, playing their guitars, trumpets and singing in Spanish, as more people started jumping into the pool and an orgy practically broke out. The whole time we had our fun, clothes coming off, water splashing everywhere, the Mariachi group played.

Girls were special to me. I wanted to date 'em all. I didn't really want to have one exclusive girl. It was like everything else in my life, I wanted to be the best. When it came to conquests, I wanted to be the best at it. I wanted to be the best drinker. Whenever a girl wanted to make me her one and only, I would leave. I don't know why. I had a better overall attitude toward life and football when I was just messing around, rather than being in a relationship. All over town, I had the reputation of being the guy you wanted at your party, because I always wanted to make sure it was the best party and everyone had fun. I showed up at a bar one night with a friend that I'd just met and each of us downed about eight Martinis. We sat there telling stories, getting to know each other and getting drunk. The bartender finally told us, "You guys probably have had about enough."

I told him, "Sure, no problem."

When we got up to leave, the bartender asked if we needed a cab. I told him, "Nope, he's right here."

And I hopped into the backseat of a cab. My new friend hopped into the front seat. He was the driver of the cab. I had taken a cab from another party and I wasn't done partying just yet, so I convinced the driver to come in and have a few drinks with me at the bar. I did that often. I wanted to make sure everyone had fun if they were with me and I always had a soft spot for people who worked long hours at thankless jobs. I tipped heavily.

Everything was getting crazier the more we won. The week of the Miami Monday Night game, my phone rang and I heard, "Hey, Dan, it's coach Pete."

It was the incompetent Bill Peterson. I thought, what the hell?

"I'm good, coach, what's up?"

"Well . . . how ya feeling about the game on Monday?"

"What do you mean?"

"Well, the spread is . . ."

I stopped him.

"Hey, coach, you know I can't talk to you about that shit. Now, come on, please don't ask me again."

I hung up the phone. I thought, man, what else could happen? And then it got even crazier.

We heard the team was going to do something special for the Monday night game against the Dolphins, but I don't think too many of us thought about it much. When I jogged onto the field for introductions, I never saw anything like it. The entire stands were blue and everyone was shaking a blue-and-white pom-poms. I thought about four years earlier when there were about 5,000 people in the stands when we lost 61-17 to the Bengals. We had the NFL stage, it was at home and we had a chip on our shoulders. Carl Mauck went on the radio the week of the game and said anyone in Houston who had a Dallas Cowboys sticker on their car should get the hell out of town. This was our chance to let everyone know we were ready for the Super Bowl. That's exactly what we did. Earl scored four touchdowns, including an 81-yarder to clinch the win. Before the season, the two favorites to come out of the AFC and make it to the Super Bowl were Pittsburgh and Miami. We beat them both on Monday night. That game pretty much pushed us into the playoffs and it was a lot of fun talking about Luv Ya Blue, which became an unofficial slogan fans talked about on radio shows, with some bringing home-made signs to games and Earl even mentioning it after the Dolphins game.

Our mood changed dramatically when we faced the Steelers at home two weeks later. I got crushed throwing the ball and immediately felt my right side crumble. I had been hit in my ribcage so often, there always were small cracks on both my sides. But this was bad. This was different. I was carted off the field, in agonizing pain, but more pissed-off that this happened to me late in the season. I broke the ninth, 10th and 12th ribs on my right side. The ninth and 10th were broken completely in half. The 12th was fractured. That Steelers game was another bloodbath. Nine players had to be carried off the field, including Earl, who hurt his groin and bruised some ribs. Mike Barber dislocated his shoulder, Elvin Bethea broke his foot, Willie Alexander fractured his jaw and Mike Renfro tore knee ligaments. For the Steelers, Lynn Swann hurt his sternum and arm, Mike Wagner busted up his knee and Loren Toews broke his ankle. It was Steelers-Oilers. That's just the way it was.

As I lay in the hospital doped up on pain-killers, telling myself I had to play in the playoffs no matter how much my ribs hurt, a guy I never saw before walked into my room and said, "Mr. Pastorini can I talk with you?"

As he walked in, I noticed he was carrying a paper bag and he was with another guy who was carrying a baseball bat. I thought, "I'm dead."

I thought they were a couple of gamblers that bet the ranch on us, lost, and came to beat my ass. I tried to reach for the buzzer to call the nurse, but I couldn't reach it because of the pain in my ribs and the pain-killers I'd taken. The guy introduced himself as Byron Donzis, as he reached into the paper bag and pulled out a kind of vest that looked like a life-preserver. He put on the vest as he kept talking about my injury and the vest, then stood there as his buddy whacked him with the bat three times, as hard as he could, directly in the ribs.

I said, "I want one of those."

Donzis was an inventor that had dabbled in several businesses, went bankrupt, made a fortune and convinced me the flak jacket would work. When I got out of the hospital, Donzis came to practice and I got fitted. The harness of the jacket was made out of a thin, lightweight Navy Seal life preserver. The rib padding was Kevlar, molded onto the life preserver, and it worked because the force of the impact was spread through little air pockets in the jacket. I started in New Orleans the next week, wearing the jacket as we clinched Houston's first NFL playoff berth with an 80-yard touchdown completion I threw to Robert Woods. We had a chance to clinch a home playoff game the final week of the season, but Dan Fouts torched us, I threw two interceptions and I got hurt again, this time popping something in my right knee. When it was announced in the Astrodome that I would return to the game, I was booed.

They called our playoff game at Miami, the "Bandage Bowl." I was fitted with a knee brace, along with the flak jacket. I had been through the 1-13 years, I wasn't about to miss our first playoff game. I was petrified that Giff would come in, have a good game and then next year I would be on the bench. It was survival for me, just like always. Plus, I had teammates that needed me and wanted me out there. There never was any question in my mind that I was going to play, although it became the biggest story of the week. People called me the toughest man in football, because of the three broken ribs, the cartilage in my knee and a strained hamstring, but I did it out of fear and insecurity. I was one play away from somebody taking my job or an injury ending it for me. I never forgot the devastating injury that Lynn Dickey suffered my second season. Plus, I had worn the flak jacket the final two games of the year and it held up so well, the NFL was talking about developing it. The jacket was making headlines across the country and Byron was getting orders from high schools and colleges, too. He told me he never would have earned so much publicity without me, so he told me I'd get 10-percent of everything his company made.

I spent the entire week in pain, but never thought for a second that I wouldn't play. Besides, I knew I could medicate myself to manage the pain and doctors were going to shoot me up before the game, anyway. When we got to Miami the day before the game, for some reason Mauck and I got separate rooms, next door to each other. Usually, we were roommates. Kickoff the next day wasn't until early evening, so I called up a girl I knew in Miami, we went out and wound up in my room. At six the next morning, I heard someone pounding on my hotel door and knew it was Mauck. The girl ran into the bathroom, as I scooped up all her clothes and threw them into the bathroom. When I opened the door, Mauck growled, "I need some toothpaste."

"OK, I'll get it," I told him. I cracked open the bathroom door, she handed me a tube of toothpaste and when I turned around I saw Mauck standing there holding up a bra with one finger.

"Shit, I thought I picked up all her clothes."

Mauck screamed, "You Dago cock-sucker! This is the most important game of our lives. You mother fucker! You can't do without screwing some bitch for one fucking night? You Dago mother fucker I'm going to fucking kill you if we lose this fucking game!"

He pounded his finger into my chest as he spoke, then turned and stormed away, cursing more. Carl and I always went to games together, early. We always rode together, were the first ones in the locker-room and just hung out. He didn't ride with me that day. When I got to the locker-room, he was the only guy in the room. He didn't look at me. He rocked back-and-forth in front of his locker, getting psyched for the game, but also still pissed off at me. He never spoke to me. I went to see Dr. Fain, who we called Doctor Pain, to get my ribs shot up. Just like he did before the New Orleans and San Diego games, Doc shot me up 12 times, using Novocaine and Marcaine. He shot me six times, twice on each rib, to deaden the area, then shot me six more times, pushing the needle between my ribs. He stuck in the needle, then turned it different directions to deaden it from the inside.

Then he put his stethoscope on my ribs.

"What are you listening for, Doc?"

"I want to see if I punctured your lung," he told me.

"Shit, Doc, how deep did you go?"

"All the way to your lung."

Usually, the pain started coming back after about an hour and a half, maybe less, so I had to get shot up at halftime, too. That was 24-shots for the game, maybe more, just like I took in New Orleans and San Diego. In case the first half dragged on or we got into an overtime game, they planned to hold some capes over me while Doc shot me up on the sidelines. When I went out for warm-ups at the Orange Bowl, everyone in the stands, all the TV and radio reporters, all the guys in the press box watched me. Everyone tried to see how I threw the ball, especially the gamblers. I just wondered if Mauck was still pissed and when we got together for 11-on-11 drills, I realized he was. He still wouldn't talk with me. Then the game started and I realized right away the Dolphins were not going to let Earl have a repeat performance of the Monday night game. They stacked everyone. They basically said they wanted me to beat them, not Earl. And I did.

When I saw them load up for Earl and bring up their safeties, I checked to pass after pass and started slinging it. I torched them. I threw for nearly 250-yards in the first-half. I kept checking to plays for Mike Barber and Kenny Burrough and they carved them up. We got to the second-half and I decided to start dealing them some Earl. Once we got the lead, Earl just pounded them. I threw for 306-yards and completed 20 out of 29 passes. It was magic.

The entire game, Mauck never said a word to me. I mean, I cut up the Dolphins in their own stadium, completed pass after pass and called a hell of a game. Not one word. He didn't say one thing after touchdowns, at halftime or on the sidelines when we met to go over things. Late in the fourth-quarter, we had a 10-point lead and we're backed up on our own 1-yard line. On fourth-down with barely 20-seconds left, I told the guys in the huddle, "Alright, we're going to take a safety."

That's when Mauck decided to start talking again.

"No! No, you crazy bastard! You check with the old man before you do that. That's stupid."

As he's chewing out my ass, Guido Merkens ran into the huddle and said, "Dan, coach says he wants you to take a safety."

I turned to Mauck and blew up.

"Is that alright with you, asshole? I call the fucking plays here. You just run what I call."

I took the snap, dropped back, killed some clock and then stepped out. We punted the ball to them with four seconds left. Ballgame. Great win.

In the locker-room afterward, I was being interviewed by more media than I'd ever seen in front of my locker-room. I stood in front of reporters wearing a towel. Mauck already was dressed and faced my locker. He handed me my shirt without saying a word. Then he handed me my deodorant, my cologne, my comb. I answered questions, laughing inside at Mauck. What the hell was he doing? Was this his way of apologizing?

I never said a damn word. He packed my bag, zipped it, put it over his shoulder. On the bus, he put the bag in the overhead and sat next to me—still without saying a word. The bus stopped at a traffic light, near a liquor store, so I shouted, "Hey, Bussy, hold it a minute. Pull over."

Before I got up to go buy some booze, Mauck yelled, "Ryno, Thompson. follow me."

Mauck jumped out of his seat and ran into the liquor store with George Reihner and Ted Thompson. I gave the cashier some money, while Mauck, Ryno and Thompson started grabbing. Mauck had two cases of beer in each hand, Ryno and Thompson each had a case of beer in each hand. When we got back on the bus, Mauck popped open a beer and handed it to me without a word. We were in traffic for 45-minutes and I was dying, laughing inside, but kept a stone face in front of Mauck. When we boarded the plane, we went to our usual seats–First Class, the last row on the left. I got the window and he got the aisle, like always. He put my bag up in the overhead, then reached over and buckled my seatbelt for me. I was shaking trying not to laugh, so I turned my head toward the window.

The plane started rolling down the runway, when Mauck finally leaned over to me.

"Hey. You think that bitch can come to New England next week?"

CHAPTER TWELVE

A doctor's needle

We crushed New England the next week. As soon as I figured out all they wanted to do was send their strong safety at me to try and bust up my ribs, I adjusted and went to the air again. Their entire gameplan was to hit me in the ribs as often as possible. Their safety Doug Beaudoin hit me square on the first three plays of the game and I thought, "Alright, you think you can take me out?"

I started calling "Bear 99" at the line, which was maximum protection. I sent Billy "White Shoes" Johnson and Kenny Burrough deep against man-to-man coverage and the Pats had no chance. They had no one who could stay with either of those guys, much less both of them. The first time I called it, I hit Kenny for a 71-yard touchdown. The Patriots fumbled on their next possession and I went right back to it when they sent the safety to hit me. I thought, "Alright, you son of a bitch, I'm going to give you more of the same."

I called 537 Z Short Post in the huddle and told Billy, "Look quick, because I'm getting it to you early."

I hit him right in the crease and he broke it long. It was easy. I threw three touchdown passes and we were up 21-0 at the half. I got shot up again at halftime and decided to start feeding them

Earl. We blew 'em out and partied hard all the way home, knowing everything was clicking and we were playing our best football.

Next up was the Steelers. Neither they nor we really wanted to go through another ferocious game like we had already played twice. But we both knew it had to be this way. We were by far their toughest opponent the previous four years, even when we didn't make the playoffs. No one played the Steelers more often or beat them more often than we had. Now, we were better than ever.

The New York Times called our AFC Championship Game in Pittsburgh, "World War III." Steelers star Joe Greene told reporters, "I would rather have played Kansas City." And when Bum was asked about another trip to Pittsburgh, he responded, "We're going to take some hospital attendants and maybe a few blood donors with us."

It turned out it wasn't a war, more like an execution. They stuffed Earl, I had a bad game and we turned the ball over nine times in slippery, icy conditions at Three Rivers Stadium. It was a total ass-whipping and it hit me hard. I barely could keep from misting up during post-game interviews, knowing I had gotten within one game of the Super Bowl and we all played horribly. Worse, when we got to the airport we were delayed for a couple of hours because of the ice and sleet. We started drowning our sorrows and by the time we took off, all three sheets were sailing. Sitting on that plane, I was devastated. As we approached Houston, the pilot came on the intercom and said, "You guys aren't going to believe this but the whole town turned out to meet you guys."

I told Carl, "Yeah, right. We lost. Nobody's going to be there."

I knew at least some people showed up, because rather than stopping the plane on the tarmac and taking buses back to the stadium like we usually did, the pilot pulled our plane up to a jetway at the main terminal. As we walked off the plane, it was an unbelievable site. It was like a sea of people parting, cheering, hollering, as we walked through the airport. There were people throughout the airport. When we got to the buses, there were people outside cheering us. I was counting on a win, so I had arranged with my secretary, Marge Mandula, to have a limousine waiting for Bum, Ted, Carl and me. We hopped in and led the caravan in our limo, down the boulevard from the airport into town. When we got onto Interstate-45, there were people parked on both sides of the road honking their horns and waving. Fans stood on the tops of their cars, cheering. As we led the buses toward the Astrodome, I rolled down my window and shouted to the police escort, "We all gotta piss."

He radioed ahead and the caravan stopped at an underpass. Bum, Carl, me and Teddy Thompson then got out, lined up side-by-side and all took a piss at the underpass on I-45, as police lights flashed and sirens blared. Then we got back in the limo and went on to the Astrodome. We rolled onto the floor of the 'Dome, the buses followed and there were 70,000 people cheering wildly, most of them holding signs or pom-pons. The scoreboard flashed lights and fireworks, cheerleaders danced and our Oilers fight song blared. It was the most amazing site I'd ever seen. It was organized by KILT Radio in Houston, but no one could have anticipated how big and amazing the rally would be. It was impromptu, sincere, passionate, uninhibited. I mean, we lost. Thousands of people lined the streets and filled the stadium on a Sunday night. And we lost.

The devastation of that loss stayed with me a long time. I wondered what the hell we had to do to beat the Steelers. I questioned whether we were good enough. Carl and Bum were my sounding board. I didn't have a wife and I didn't bother my family, because I didn't like them to worry about me, especially my mom. She worried about me a lot. I had a lot of talks with King Hill in the off-season, too. I finally met with Bum at the facility.

"Maybe it's time you play the kid," I told Bum. "Maybe it's time to move on."

"Dan, you played your ass off. It was just one of those games. Don't worry about that stuff some people say. They don't know."

"I'm tired of it, Bum."

I was hell-bent on leaving. I was tired of getting blamed every time we lost, while anytime something went right it was Earl, Bum and everybody else but me who got the credit. I had my house vandalized while I was out one night. Somebody broke a window and spray-painted some shit about me on the fence. I realized that's the life of a quarterback in the NFL, but it just seemed I was a lightning rod. People either loved me or hated me, there was no in-between. I brought a lot of it on myself, because I never bull-shit or played games. It wasn't just my imagination or insecurity. I know what I felt, what I heard and I couldn't deal with it anymore. I loved every one of those players in the locker-room. I just thought maybe it was time to give Gif his chance and move on.

"Do something for me," Bum finally said. "Work hard. Let's get there again next year. Take us there again and if you still feel the same, I'll trade you anywhere you want to go."

I agreed, we shook hands and that was good enough for me. About a week later, I was shopping near the Galleria and reached to open the door at Joske's, a big new department store in town. As I stretched my right arm to push open the door, it went numb and completely limp. It just dropped and I couldn't lift it. I thought for a second I was having a stroke, it just had no strength in it at all. Nothing. I felt a twinge in my right rib cage and shoulder and realized something happened to the nerves on my entire right upper-body. When I got home, I tried throwing a ball and the furthest I could throw it was about 15-feet.

I was terrified. Was that it? That's how my career ends? I went to see Bum and then doctors did all kinds of different tests. Sure enough, when Doc shot me up, he damaged the nerve that controls the Serratus Anterior muscle. The sole purpose of this nerve and the Serratus Anterior is to move your shoulder blade. They call it the "boxer's" muscle, because without it, a boxer couldn't throw a punch. It basically helps your arm sling forward after you cock it back. It was severely damaged. Whenever I threw a football at my best, I brought my arm back unusually far, almost parallel to the ground behind me. When the doctor asked me to take my arm back like I would on a normal throw, I couldn't take it past my ear.

After all those years getting tattooed by everyone from Dick Butkus, to Deacon Jones, to "Mean" Joe Greene and Jack Lambert, this is what ends my career? A doctor's needle? From my rookie year until I walked off the field in Pittsburgh a few weeks earlier, I had suffered 12 concussions. I broke my nose 16 times. I broke my cheekbone. I cracked my sternum. I broke my collar bone twice. I separated my right shoulder four times and my left shoulder six times. I had two operations on my right shoulder and four on my left. I fractured four transverse processes in my back. I had some kind of fractures in my ribs 38-times. I had staph infection in my elbow. I couldn't count all the broken thumbs and fingers. But this was different. This was my arm and I couldn't throw a football.

After all the shitty years to get to the doorstep of the Super Bowl, I was on the brink of losing it all. I started doing everything I could to strengthen my arm and shoulder, and flex it again. Our trainer Jerry Miens built a brace for me that was like a fake scapula. It basically held my wing in place with an elastic band, so it helped me move my arm forward when I cocked it back. It was the only way I could throw. My shoulder was paralyzed without it. I never really lifted weights before, but Joe Bugel put me on a weight program and I was in there every day, building up muscle. I spent a lot of time worrying if I ever would get that zip back on the ball. I took a lot of pride in how I threw the football. I always looked at the flight of the ball in the air and could see the zip on it. But as the 1979 season approached, even as I started throwing the ball again, the zip just wasn't there. I was in total survival mode and fighting all kinds of personal worries beyond football.

When I signed the contract before the '78 season, dad asked me to help out he and mom. He had his second heart bypass operation early in the year and had to let the restaurant go. He got a job working at Riverside Country Club in the food services department, but needed help with monthly bills. I also was paying child support to June. If I couldn't play anymore, how was I going to help them? I tried to do as many things as I could outside of football, building contacts and possibilities for the future. Bud Adams made me feel even more alienated, when I met with him and asked if I could restructure my contract, so I could help my parents more easily. I didn't ask for a penny more on the contract. I just wanted a little less money deferred and about $15,000 paid during the contract's term. Bud told me he couldn't do it. He never gave me a reason, he just said no. I felt beaten down physically, weathered, and wondered again if Bud really wanted me around anymore. Fortunately, I was able to get away as far as I could.

I had hosted a celebrity tennis tournament before the '78 season and the casting agent Jack Gilardi got a lot of Hollywood types to come participate–Telly Savalas, Dick Van Patton, Farrah Fawcett. Gilardi and I got to be pretty good friends. After the '78 season, Gilardi got me a role in a movie called Killer Fish. The movie was shot in Brazil at a place called Angra dos Reis. I figured, what the hell? Reporters always described me as having, "matinee idol" looks, and I'd done a bad movie before, so why not? Maybe there's a future there. I played Hans, an escape artist, and being on a big-time movie set with actors like Lee Majors, Karen Black, Margaux Hemmingway and James Franciscus was exciting. Franciscus and I hit it off pretty good. The cast stayed in little hotel cabins along the waterfront and built a bonfire on the beach almost every night. It was an open party for anybody that wanted to come. There were several small islands off the shore of Angra dos Reis and everyone knew Hollywood had come to Brazil. Before long, the most amazing tall, blonde-haired, blue-eyed girls started showing up at the bonfires. They were the kids of German

World War II refugees, living in Brazil. They were the "supreme race" science projects, and they all were drop-dead gorgeous. They came over every night to party with us and they were classy, reserved, young and beautiful women.

I got along best with Jim Franciscus, he was just a regular guy, down to earth and didn't take himself so seriously like a lot of Hollywood-types. One girl we met invited Jim and me to her dad's house and we water-skied, had some drinks and just partied. When it was time to leave, I decided to ski back to the beach while they rode on the boat. I stepped off the dock and told the boat's driver to hit it, but I miss-timed my jump and popped my right hamstring. I tore two of the three origins of the hamstring muscle at the top of my leg, to the point I could stick my fist into the place where the muscle pulled off. It was immediately black-and-blue, excruciating and I was pissed off, because here was something else I needed to start rehabbing.

We did a lot of waiting and sitting around, waiting for scenes to get shot. It got long and boring as hell. We had a few days off before the Fourth Of July, so as we sat on the beach one night, I asked Franciscus, "You want to go to Baytown?"

"Where?"

"Baytown . . . Texas."

Here we were in South America and all of a sudden I had this random idea to go to a little town east of Houston, known mostly for its oil and gas refineries. Franciscus said, "What the hell? Let's go."

We caught a flight to Miami, caught a connection into Houston and then got a ride to Baytown with my friend, Larry Enderli. We spent the weekend at Baytown's Fourth Of July festival and partied a couple days, with Enderli in awe the whole time we were there.

"I can't believe you guys. That's James Franciscus walking around Baytown! I can't believe this."

We caught a plane back to South America and finished filming. I never was certain why I always did things that just felt right at the time. Sometimes it got me into trouble and I asked myself, are these things happening to me or am I allowing them to happen to me? I realized I was insecure and often dealt with it by putting up a front or acting on my first instinct and whatever happened, happened.

I never said anything about my arm problems before the '79 season, but it was obvious to everyone that something was wrong. I was horrible the first half of the season and everyone was criticizing me, with good reason, and questioning whether I had lost it. I completed just 12-of-30 passes in our season-opener against Washington. I completed just four passes against Pittsburgh and just five passes against Baltimore the sixth game of the year. Through six games I had just four touchdown passes and 12 interceptions.

A reporter named Dale Robertson from the Houston Post kept writing a bunch of shit about how all the years had caught up to me, the injuries were keeping me down and I couldn't throw the ball anymore. I finally had enough and just reacted. I read something he wrote about me, threw the paper in his face when I saw him in the locker-room and told him, "Why are you doing this shit? You're messing with my bread and butter. I'd like to keep this a secret from people. You don't help by broadcasting it around the league that my arm's screwed up and I'm not playing well. Everyone can see that I'm not playing well. I'm never going to talk to you again, Dale. When you first got here I was one of the few people in the locker-room who talked with you. But I'm done with this shit."

We went to Seattle in late-October and got our asses kicked to drop to 4-3 for the year. People all over the league wondered if my arm was dead and we could recover from the slow start. That trip to Seattle was the Brownie Game.

A few weeks earlier, I was a celebrity chef at a huge charity gala at the Rockets' arena, The Summit. Teams of celebrities cooked their favorite recipes for charitable donations and I was teamed with my neighbor, Barry Warner, who worked at one of the hottest radio stations in town, KIKK. It was a huge event, with the highest-end society types and business people invited. I made my Chicken Pastorini, which was a recipe from mom and dad's restaurant and was outstanding. Barry made cream cheese brownies. But for some stupid reason, Barry decided to make two batches—one regular and the other laced with enough marijuana to get an elephant high. I don't know why Barry decided to make his special brownies right there in the middle of The Summit, but he did. As he let the special brownies cool, he turned to get the other brownies out of the oven and an elderly society lady grabbed one of the ones that were laced with marijuana.

"Oh, ma'am, you can't have one of those!" Barry said, trying to grab it out of her hand. "Those are for another event."

The blue-hair pulled the old, "Do you know who I am thing?" on Barry, so when she finished rambling on about how her family helped found the city of Houston, Barry responded, "Well, I'm sorry. Have another brownie, then." The poor lady was a mess during the auction, laughing uncontrollably, then slumping in her chair, falling asleep, until finally her husband took her home.

Before the Seattle trip, I was feeling horrible about the season I was having, even though my arm was starting to feel better. I saw Barry after practice and told him, "Super Jew, it's a long trip to Seattle. I think you need to bake."

When I got to the back of the plane and saw Barry, I asked him, "Are these the leaded or the unleaded?"

He just smiled, so I started eating the brownie. Bum walked back there and before I could tell Barry to put them away, Bum said, "Hey, brownies!" and he grabbed one. I covered my face, walked away and Bum grabbed another one. Everyone at the back of the plane just snickered. After we checked into the hotel in Seattle, at our regular pre-game meeting, Bum was woozy. He started writing on the chalk board, then stopped and said, "Ah, hell. You guys know this stuff. Let's just call it a day."

CHAPTER THIRTEEN

Just get us to Pittsburgh

It was an ongoing thing to keep my arm and shoulder strong, but after the Seattle game my arm came back just about full strength. My passes had more zip, people had to respect our passing game again and we went on a four-game win streak heading into Dallas for a Thanksgiving Day showdown with the Cowboys. Next to getting to the Super Bowl, nothing was bigger in Houston than beating the Cowboys. Carl talked all week about how much he hated the Cowboys and anyone in Houston who like them should leave town. Bud Adams wanted it. Bum wanted it badly. Two years earlier when we played the Cowboys in a damn preseason game, after we lost, Bum kept saying, "Anybody but the Cowboys. Anybody but the Cowboys."

During the week, Bum kept telling us, "Fellas, this is just another game. Prepare like you always prepare." Before the game in the locker-room, he told us again, "Don't believe everything you've been hearing. It only counts one if we win or we lose."

We played a hell of a game in Dallas. Earl ran his ass off right at the Cowboys, until they just started sending Cliff Harris on every snap to crush Earl. I could barely get my hand out from handing the ball off and Cliff Harris was smashing him. Bum said to keep running Earl, but finally in the fourth-quarter as we trailed I got into the huddle and said, "Screw this. Let's run a post, Kenny."

I hit Kenny Burrough with a 32-yard touchdown pass and as I walked past Bum on the sideline I said, "I'm not going to kill this kid, Bum."

He said, "That's OK. I'll take seven-points."

After the game, Bum said, "Dallas may be America's Team, but we're Texas' team. And I wouldn't have it any other way."

As I stood in front of my locker celebrating and answering questions, Kenny Burrough shouted at me from a phone in the trainers' room.

"Hey, Dante, it's for you."

"Just a minute," I told him.

"No, really. You need to come get the phone."

"Who is it?"

"Farrah Fawcett."

Yeah, right. I stood there in a towel, in front of all these media guys, shaking my head, as if Farrah was on the phone. Somebody must have put Burrough up to it.

"No shit, Dante. Come here!"

I picked up the phone still thinking it was a joke.

"Hello."

I heard Farrah's distinctive, sweet voice. I met her at my celebrity tennis tournament, but it was just exchanging pleasantries and thanking her for coming.

"Well, I was just in town for Thanksgiving with some family and I was hoping we could go to dinner or something," she told me.

We talked a little more, she gave me her number and when I turned around, everybody in the locker-room looked at me like, really? Farrah Fawcett? We started dating and it got pretty serious, pretty quickly. Farrah came into town a few times, we'd go out, play tennis, have dinner and it just became a relationship. She basically was doing with me what I'd done for years with other women. It didn't take long for my secretary, Marge, to start telling me, "Don't fall in love with her, Dan. She's using you. You're the flavor of the month."

Marge took a lot of Farrah's calls for me and started telling me every move Farrah made before Farrah even made them. Marge didn't think I should trust her.

We played the Steelers on Monday Night Football the second-to-last game of the year in 1979. It was the official debut of the Luv Ya Blue placards. Every fan in the stadium had one of those signs, as well as pompoms. The city was berserk for the Oilers and this was the showcase game of the year. Writers called Pittsburgh's defense the greatest in NFL history. They called the game a preview of an AFC Championship Game rematch from 1978. And that night, we had their number. We put Timmy Wilson in front of Joe Greene on every play, because Joe always took out the guard and center, to allow Jack Lambert to run free. So we had Wilson run through that gap on every snap and just smash Lambert. They never adjusted to it and we wore out Lambert's ass. He was one of the best linebackers, ever. He could play for me anytime. But by the third-quarter, with Wilson pounding him on every snap, his tongue was hanging out.

The atmosphere was electric. Frank Gifford said on ABC during the game, "This city has embraced a professional team like I've never seen before."

Howard Cosell said, "You are seeing pro football at its best tonight. You're looking at the two best teams in football. Ladies and gentleman, this is the best that the National Football League has to offer."

I threw a rocket to Kenny Burrough for our first touchdown, probably the best throw I'd made in a year. We were leading 20-17 and driving deep on the Steelers again with just a few seconds left, when I called timeout. Howard and Fran Tarkenton started giving me a hard time on the air about trying to rub it in the Steelers' noses. But that's not why I called timeout. I broke the huddle ready to take a knee, but realized we may need the points to win a tiebreaker against the Steelers, so we could have home field advantage in the playoffs. I sure as hell didn't want to go up to Pittsburgh again, so I called timeout and started walking toward our bench, when Bum told me, "I know what you're thinking, but it isn't going to make a difference. Just fall on the ball."

Everybody in the huddle knew what I was doing, too, but Joe Greene kept yelling at me from across the line of scrimmage. He didn't even get in a stance. He just pointed at me.

"Go ahead, Dan. Try to score. I'm going to let you score. And I'm gonna knock the shit out of you on national television."

As I lined up to take the snap, I said, "Joe, I'm going to fall on it, I'm going to fall on it!"

He kept pointing at me, then put his hands on his hips as I took the snap. When I fell on the ball, he picked me up and said, "I knew you weren't going to score."

"Goddammit, Joe, you scared the hell out of me!"

He just laughed and said, "Seeya in Pittsburgh."

I knew the Steelers defensive guys real well. I played in a couple of all-star games with Jack Hamm, Andy Russell and I became friends my second year in the league when we took a road trip with a sponsor and Lambert, I respected him a lot. Joe Greene, L.C. Greenwood and those guys on the defensive line were in another class. I knew all about the Fearsome Foursome. I knew all about the Purple People Eaters and Doomsday Defense, but you haven't lived until you've gone against the Steel Curtain. There were very few games against the Steelers where I was able to walk off the field on my own. They just beat me to shit. But as badly as I wanted to beat those guys, I respected them and I know they respected us.

Before we could see Mean Joe and the boys again in Pittsburgh, we had to get through Denver in the wildcard game, then San Diego. The Broncos game changed everything, even though we won. I ruptured my groin scrambling out of the pocket. It was completely torn, with the purple and black bruise going all the way down my leg. Earl seriously hurt his groin muscle, too, and Kenny Burrough hurt his back and hip. We were such heavy underdogs heading to San Diego, Las Vegas didn't even post a point-spread. We went in with the back-up quarterback, back-up running back and Mike Renfro carrying the receiving corps. Worse, Robbie Carpenter broke his ankle on a fall during practice. He was on crutches the morning of the game and didn't even take an aspirin. Bum said, "If we run out of players, we'll just punt and play defense."

Robbie just taped his ankle up tight and ran all over the Chargers. Giff called a hell of a game, Vernon Perry, a typical Bum kind of player who came from the Canadian League, picked off four passes and blocked a field-goal. It was the most inspirational game I ever saw and the most courageous I ever saw from Robbie. It was unbelievable the courage everyone showed on the field. There never was a better team effort in league history. Something truly special happened on the field that day. It was a product of all those days and nights we spent together, all those times we fought for each other, coming together from all sorts of different places, with all sorts of different backgrounds. The whole time I was on the sideline watching, as we built momentum and took control, I kept telling myself, "Just get us to Pittsburgh. Just get us to Pittsburgh. And this time, we'll beat those damn guys."

The week of the Steelers game, reporters came from all over the country to preview the most anticipated rematch in football. There were TV cameras, magazine guys, reporters from out of town. A sportswriter from Pittsburgh, John Clayton, was interviewing Bum outside about his unique way of bringing a team together when I was called into the media room.

I walked into the locker-room reading the paper and saw several quotes attributed to me by Dale Robertson. I found Dale and took him into a back room, so we could talk.

"If you don't talk directly to me, don't quote me, Dale. You stabbed me in the back."

I threw the newspaper at him and walked away. He followed me through the training room, through the locker-room and toward the back door into the press room, where I was going to talk with the media.

He told me, "Is it alright if I get your quotes here, you fucking prima donna asshole?"

I turned toward him and every camera in the room turned toward me. I was challenged in front of the entire room. I told myself, "You know what? We're going to go outside and dance a little bit."

I grabbed Dale by the shirt, picked him up and shoved him through the door. As I shoved him, he tripped, fell back and rolled down some stairs to the back of the facility. That's where Bum was talking with John Clayton. Bum was telling Clayton how much he loved coaching our team, how the city loved us and we loved the city. Dale's head hit Bum's boot. I stepped on Dale's chest and told him, "If you write another thing about me, I'm going to fucking kill you."

Bum didn't skip a beat. As we were rolling out the door, Bum was telling Clayton, "This group just gets along real well . . ."

Then he looked at us on the ground, turned to Clayton and said, ". . . 'til now."

Across the country there were headlines like, "Pastorini attacks writer" and "Pastorini assaults reporter." The next day when I got to practice, Carl, Ted Thompson and Mike Reinfeldt taped the outline of a body, including Dale's big afro haircut, on the ground where I pushed him. They got one of our trainers to get a No. 7 practice jersey with "Rocky" printed on the back of the jersey and that's what I wore to practice.

I spent the week answering questions about the incident, listening to fans rave on about it on the radio and trying to get well and figure out a way to beat the Steelers. I scouted myself, trying to find my own tendencies, so I could go against them in the game and give them different looks. I treated my groin every day, wrapped it, took pills. There was no way I was going to miss the AFC Championship. I never was more confident we would go into Pittsburgh and beat them. None of us were awed by the environment, the weather, the Steelers, nothing. Bum said before the game, "No excuses. Earl's running at full-speed and Dan's running at half-speed, but Dan's never been very fast, anyway."

Doc Pain wanted to shoot up my groin, but I told him no. I decided I would take two or three Darvon every quarter. It was cold and slippery and hard-hitting as ever. It became obvious to me Earl in fact wasn't running at full-speed and the Steel Curtain had adjusted to the way we ran Timmy Wilson at Jack Lambert in our Monday night win. They were absolutely stuffing Earl. He was getting nothing, rushing for less than ten yards by halftime. I could hardly move. I was a statue back there, limping when I dropped back, but I went into the huddle in the third-quarter and said, "Alright, guys, we're gonna have to throw this thing."

I just decided, screw it, I'm taking this game. It's on me. And we immediately took momentum and started driving down the field. They were winning 17-10 when we got down to their goal-line. I called an audible, 99, which was a meet-me-in-the-corner type of flair. It was one of those passes I could do in my sleep. I'd made that throw perfectly with my eyes closed before. I saw Mike Renfro get even with Ron Johnson, so I dropped it in there and he made a hell of a catch. Renfro immediately jumped up celebrating a touchdown. The side judge, Donald Orr, trailed the play and didn't signal a touchdown. I turned to referee Jim Tunney and told him, "Get it right, Jim." Everyone surrounded Orr telling him to get the call right. Bum threw up his hands, screaming, touchdown, touchdown. The entire stadium and millions watching on TV saw Renfro catch the ball well inbounds and get both feet inbounds. Tunney met with his crew and came out to signal, incomplete. We finally had the Steelers on their heels, in their house and it got taken away. It ripped my guts out. I mean, it killed me inside. We wound up settling for a field-goal and we lost all momentum. That play changed everything. They dared us to throw the ball and we threw it right at them. If they would have made the right call, we would have had control and maybe they would have re-thought stacking up against Earl. It was a killer.

I walked off the field after the Steelers beat us, with my elbow bruised and bleeding, my groin and entire left leg throbbing and a pain in my stomach from taking a shot and losing my wind. Dwight White walked off on one side of me and Joe Greene on the other. Joe told me, "You guys did get screwed on that call."

I patted Joe on the back of the head and told him, "Well, go win it for us."

We were delayed again leaving Pittsburgh. I went to the back of the plane and just wanted to be alone. I sat in the jump seat at the back of the plane with all the flight attendants that always took care of us. Jackie, Kathy, the whole bunch. They weren't just flight attendants. They were nurses.

I was tired of everything. I was tired of always taking flak. I was tired of always hurting. I was tired of losing for so many years. I barely could walk in Pittsburgh. I was beat up. I was drained. I thought to myself, "How the hell do we beat those guys without killing them? Do we have to go out there with guns and shoot 'em?"

We played the Steelers two and three times a year for all those years. Those two games, those two championship games, those were the true Super Bowls. We were the two best teams in the NFL, but we had nothing to show for it. They had Super Bowl rings.

I drank a couple of scotches and a few beers, drowning my sorrows at the back of the plane. I sank lower and lower in my seat, then looked up and saw Bum walking down the aisle toward me.

"Ah, shit," I said. "No. Not now."

Bum walked up to me, looked me dead in the eye and said, "Daniel, I'm really proud of you. You played like a warrior. You played hurt. You did everything I asked you to do. Do you still feel like you did last year? Do you still want to be traded?"

I exhaled, paused, looked at him and said, "Yeah. Yeah, I do. It's probably best for everybody. Play Giff. Trade me. Do what's best for the team."

"Well," Bum said, "you're a man of your word. You played your ass off. I'll trade you. Where do you want to go?"

"Anywhere on the West Coast."

It hurt Bum when I told him I wanted to be traded, I could see it in his eyes. I think he wanted me to say, no. He wanted me to say that I wanted to make another run at the Steelers. And deep down, I did. I wanted to beat those guys and I wanted to do it with the guys on that plane. But I just said what I felt.

I had a limousine waiting for us again when we landed in Houston. Bum and I got into the same limousine, with Mauck and Thompson. Bum and I were the only ones who knew this would be our last ride together. The roads were packed again with fans honking their horns, hanging over bridges, waving, yelling. The Astrodome was beyond capacity and there were 20,000 people outside stuck in traffic. It was a bigger and crazier scene than the year before, which I thought I never would see again. I rode around the 'Dome on the back of a police motorcycle, then got on stage and sat behind Bum when he got up to address the crowd. I had my elbows on my knees, thinking, "Am I doing the right thing? Will I be better off? Yes, I will. No, I won't." The Gemini in me was roaring.

Then Bum uttered one of the most memorable lines in NFL history.

"Last year, we knocked on the door. This year, we banged on the door. Next year, we're gonna kick that sumbitch in."

I looked up to the roof of the Astrodome, looked around at the crowd and said to myself, "Not with me."

Bum traded me to the Raiders for Ken Stabler.

CHAPTER FOURTEEN

A lost soul

When I got traded, the headline the next day blared, "Pastorini can make passes at Farrah in Hollywood."

No one really understood why I left. It was simple. I was miserable. For nine years I tried to get those guys and that city a winner. When we got a winner, I tried to get to a Super Bowl. They never got there with me and I was tired of being told I was the problem. So if I was the problem, I wanted a change. Maybe they could get there without me. Going to the West Coast had nothing to do with chasing a career in Hollywood or Farrah. I thought I could go home again, plus my daughter Brahna was in California, so I could actually see her more often. I became even more introspective and critical of myself as I faced the reality of leaving. I was banged up and beat up emotionally and physically. I packed up my apartment, hopped into my Porsche and turned on the radio as I headed west on Interstate-10. I turned on a sports talk show and heard everybody talking about the trade. One of the hosts declared, "Well, we finally got rid of Pastorini. I've got two things to say about Dante: Goodbye and good riddance."

I turned off the radio, stuck my right hand out of the sun roof, stepped on the gas, shot the finger into the air and said, "Screw you, Houston."

Farrah and I spent less time together after we lost to the Steelers, including at the Super Bowl in Los Angeles. During the week, we went out just twice. We planned to spend a lot of time together at the Super Bowl, but she was divorcing Lee Majors and dating Ryan O'Neal. Still, Farrah and I had become very close. Not many people knew how serious we were. My last night there, she came over for a Nooner and before she left, she jumped on top of me, gave me a big kiss and said, "I can't wait to see you tonight."

When I walked into the bathroom after she left, I saw that she wrote on the mirror in red lipstick, "I want to have your baby."

But Farrah didn't return my calls that night. I didn't hear from her the rest of the week, or the next. Or ever. One minute she wanted to have my baby, the next she was gone. My secretary Marge had her pegged from the start. Marge told me Farrah just wanted to screw around with me, but Ryan O'Neal was better for her career. Marge probably was right about that, too. Farrah had no conscience.

Not long after I got to Oakland, I got a call from Ira Ritter, the publisher of Playgirl Magazine. I guessed he saw me in the tabloids with Farrah. He asked if I would do a spread in Playgirl. One of my receivers with the Raiders, Bobby Chandler, dared me to do it and I figured, why not? Joe Namath did a spread in Cosmopolitan and Burt Reynolds did Playgirl, so I told Ira I would do it, but I didn't want frontal shots published. It was just one of those decisions that sounded good at the time and was a big seller on the newsstands. When it came out, I had hundreds of them sent to me by women to autograph. But I did it mostly just because of ego. I didn't want to be out-done by someone else.

I caught hell in the locker-room and I don't think it sat well with Al, but I was just reacting like I always did, being Hollywood because it felt right.

I heard all the stories about Al Davis. I knew some players loved him and others hated him. I heard that he and Kenny Stabler didn't speak for a year before the Raiders traded Snake. I heard that he played favorites and could be prone to mood swings and temper tantrums. My kind of guy, I figured. But when I was learning the offense, getting to know the players and looking for a place to live I didn't see any of that.

Al was a prince to me. He showed me around the facility, introduced me to people in the organization and put me up at the Hyatt Regency until I could find a place. He called just about every day to ask if everything was OK or if I needed anything. I stayed at the Hyatt for three months. He got me a car to drive and paid for everything, including meals. He called and asked how I was picking up the offense, if I needed a realtor, if I'm getting around the city OK. I thought, "This guy isn't anything like I thought he would be."

I finally asked Al if he could help me with something that had been weighing on my mind. I asked him the same thing I asked Bud Adams. With their restaurant closed and entering their retirement years, mom and dad were struggling with money. I had been giving them $1,500 a month, but I didn't want that to put a strain on my finances. I told Al about my parents' predicament and asked if I could re-do my contract, so I could get more money up-front and less deferred.

"How much would take care of what you're paying your parents?"

"Probably $15,000 or maybe $20,000," I told him.

"Let's do $50,000, to make sure."

He re-did the contract in just a couple of days, adding $50,000 to my salary and deferring $50,000 less. Just like that, it was done.

When Bum traded me to the Raiders, sportswriters all over the country said Al and I would be a match made in heaven. I had my rebellious side, spoke my mind and had a temper, but Al didn't care about any of that. All he cared about was winning. And I had that lightning bolt for a right arm, which fit in perfectly with the way Al liked his teams to stretch the field. My throws maybe didn't have the same zip they once had, but I still had a better arm than most quarterbacks in the league. Al wanted the vertical passing game and I was his guy. Cliff Branch could out-run a lot of coverages, so if I threw the ball out to him, he'd go get it. Perfect fit.

Jim Plunkett was my backup and I always felt the resentment from him; an uneasiness. For the first time since we were in high school, I was picked in front of him and it wasn't an easy pill for him to swallow. Jim was a fragile guy. He went through a lot of shit in New England, just like I did in Houston and Archie did in New Orleans. I finally produced when I got a good team around me in Houston, but Plunkett never produced and had a big chip on his shoulder. He was just a sensitive guy.

Training camp went well for me. I was hungry to get back to the AFC Championship Game and lo and behold, one of the first faces I saw at camp was referee Jim Tunney, who didn't have the balls to make the right call in Pittsburgh. Jim visited us for an annual rules seminar. The big change he talked about was the possibility of the league going to instant-replay to make correct calls. He said the league was talking about it and testing instant-replay during the preseason. I sat there, just disgusted looking at Tunney, as he talked about how replay might work, how it would be tested and eventually how it would be implemented. Then he showed a video of a, "potential reviewable call." It was the throw I made to Renfro against the Steelers.

"Are you shitting me?" I hollered.

I raised my hand and Tunney looked at me, bothered, but took my question.

"Was he inbounds, Jim?"

"No, he wasn't. He didn't have possession."

"Well you're the only one who thinks so, Jim."

He refused to ever admit he blew that call. Every other referee on the field that day saw replays, said Mike was in, and apologized. Some of them apologized to me personally. It was a catch. The league said it was a blown call. That was the entire reason Jim was up there talking about instant replay. But he was a cocky son of a bitch that refused to ever admit he was wrong.

We opened the regular-season against Kansas City and absolutely swarmed them. I threw for 317-yards and a couple of touchdowns and could have thrown for 400. It was easy. It was pitch-and-catch, and I did feel like the Raiders and I were a match made in heaven. The next week at San Diego, I hit Branch for a long touchdown bomb and that's when I realized just how fast he was. I was trying to throw the ball away, but he put it into another gear and ran under it. By the end of the day, though, I threw a couple of picks, hyperextended my knee, missed a few plays and we lost in overtime. The next week we beat the Redskins, but I threw three picks. The home fans in Oakland were booing me. Walking off the field with Joe Theisman after the game, Joe told me, "Man, we played you in Houston and they booed you. Now they don't like you here, either?"

I just laughed and shook my head, but it was a rude awakening. I replaced the Messiah out there when I took over for Kenny Stabler. Nothing I did was right, even when we won. I limped through a pretty bad game at Buffalo on my hurt knee and then at home against the Chiefs, Gino Mangiero crashed into the bottom of my knee as I released a pass. I broke my right tibia plateau. It snapped clean and went into my knee. I couldn't straighten my leg; the bones were just sort of locked together. As I lay there, grabbing my leg, trying not to scream, I heard fans booing me. When they carried me off the field, more fans were booing and it was louder. My father was in the stands, crying. I wasn't Kenny Stabler, which meant I had no chance replacing him.

Two days later, I had surgery at Cedars Sinai Hospital in Los Angeles. The surgeon straightened my leg and put it in a cast. I spent three days in the hospital and the doctor told me it would take six to eight weeks to heal. I got a few calls from teammates and Coach Tom Flores while I was in the hospital. Al called me once, but didn't say much, just, "Tough break."

When I got back to Oakland, I went to the practice facility to see the trainers and my teammates. I walked into the locker-room on crutches just as practice had started. When I turned the corner from the training room into the locker-room, I saw Al across the locker-room, about 50-feet away from me.

"Mr. Davis, how ya doing?"

He didn't say a word. He just glanced up at me and kept walking toward me, down the center of the locker-room, turning his head side-to-side, looking into every locker. He did this all the time and I never was quite sure why. He was either making sure no one was late to practice, or just snooping into every player's locker. But it was as if I wasn't even in the room. He just totally ignored me. As I stood there, he kept walking toward me not acknowledging that I even was there. He walked to within 10-feet of me and I said loudly, "Hey, Al! How ya doing?"

He stopped, looked at me and just kind of exhaled and shook his head with a look of complete disgust on his face. It was as if I was some kind of piece of meat that wasn't any use to him anymore. I was waste. He walked right past me, so close that he almost brushed one of my crutches and didn't say a word. My mind started racing, thinking all kinds of things. Is he trying to send me some kind of message? Is this some kind of game?

As he walked past I shouted, "Hey, mother-fucker, what's your problem?"

He stopped, turned around and looked at me like I was a piece of trash. He looked at me like I wasn't even worth the dirt on the bottom of his shoes.

I walked out to practice with my head scrambled. What kind of game was Al playing? I realized this was just the kind of man he was. He's petty. He throws trash away. To him, I wasn't a man or a human being. I was trash because I broke my tibia.

I thought to myself, if that's the game he wanted to play, by God, let's dance you son of a bitch. I started busting my ass trying to get my leg back in shape. I drank two gallons of milk a day. I massaged my leg, took calcium pills, Vitamin C. I sat at night watching TV, flexing my leg inside my cast, trying to keep the muscles active. Four weeks later before we played the Dolphins at home, the team doctor said he wanted to examine my leg. They cut off the cast and took an X-ray. When the doctor looked at the X-ray, he looked at me, then looked at the technician and told him, "Now go take a picture of his right leg."

"That is his right leg."

"No, it's not. Take it again," Doc told him.

The doctor stood there as the technician took another X-ray and when he looked at it again, he said, "I'll be damn. You're healed. The bone looks great."

He told me to start some light workouts and stay away from impact stuff. I started working out almost all day, every day. Two weeks later, I was running three miles a day, cutting in both directions on my leg, dropping back, making throws.

I went to Al and asked if I could be activated and get back with the team. He told me to talk with Tom Flores. I went to Tom's office and he told me to check with Al.

"Wait a minute, Tom. What's going on here?"

"Well, it's not my call, Dan," he told me.

I went back to Al and asked him why I couldn't be activated and he said, "We just can't do it right now."

We were winning. Plunkett wasn't playing great, but we were winning and since everyone knew Plunkett was a pretty fragile guy, Al didn't want Plunkett looking over his shoulder. I told Tom, "I didn't ask for my starting job. I didn't ask for anything but to get back with the team and start practicing and get ready in case something happened to Plunkett and you need me."

Al never said a damn word about our little locker-room exchange. He never had to. I was shit to him because somebody else was winning and I didn't put up with his bullshit. I just threw up my hands.

I totally retreated from the team and started drinking more, harder, and more often. We went to Philadelphia three weeks later and just like every week, I went through the same drill. I asked Tom to activate me. He said no. It was as if I was dead to all of them. I was on an island. Ted Hendricks brought a bottle of whiskey on the plane to Philly and I drank almost the whole bottle by myself. I was drunk and pissed off. As we got off the plane, somehow I wound up standing right behind Al. He turned around and I stared him right in the face. I put up both my fists like an old bare-knuckle fighter, did a little Muhammad Ali-shuffle dance and told him, "Hey, mother-fucker, activate me."

That didn't set too well. Al got in my face and guys had to grab me and pull me away from Al. He started cussing me out and called me a worthless drunk. I retreated even further after that. I was a lost soul. I had never been in that position before in my life. I never could control much in my life, but I always could prove myself on the field and suddenly I wasn't even allowed to step foot on the field. I wasn't a part of the team. I didn't feel a part of anything. I just drowned myself in whiskey.

I regretted my decision with Bum. I wondered if Bum really wanted to keep me at all, or had I not said anything, would Bum have made the decision to trade me anyway? I drank most all day and went out every night. It was an embarrassment. I knew I was wrong. There was no justification for the drinking I did. But

I knew what I was feeling and I was miserable. I felt as if I was losing my life.

Tom called me into his office and asked what the hell I could have been thinking challenging Al like I did in front of the entire team.

"I'm sorry, Tom. I lost my head, but I'm pissed off that I can't play. Yeah, I had too much to drink and I broke training. What are you going to do, deactivate me?"

"Just take it easy, Dan, we're winning right now. You know how it is with the boss," Tom told me.

I said, "Ask anyone that's ever played with me. I'm all about the team, Tom. I'm not asking for my job back. I want to help. I want some reps. I want some practice. I'm sitting around with my thumb up my ass and you're going with a rookie quarterback backing up Plunkett?"

Tom was an OK guy, but I didn't appreciate that he didn't go to bat for me. He knew I should have been activated. Marc Wilson had never taken a snap in the NFL and that's the guy they wanted backing up Plunkett? I was healthy. I was making every throw. Someone finally challenged Al on the little horseshit games he liked to play and I got ostracized for it. I was black-listed. Other players started noticing it. They knew Al was all about beating the other guy and right now I was that other guy. He wanted to beat me down. Al started spreading all kinds of rumors about me around the league, too–that I had drug problems, that I was damaged. The incident on the plane was my death certificate as far as Al Davis was concerned and I never was allowed to go on another road-trip until we got to the Super Bowl.

We made the playoffs as a wild-card team. Our first game was against the Oilers at the Coliseum and that only made me feel more detached. My entire life I had been a part of a team and I never was more proud than to put on that Oilers uniform with those guys. I screwed up leaving Houston and I screwed up in Oakland. By the time the Oilers got to Oakland, I had been drinking hard, going out every night. The night before the game, I went to the Hyatt Regency where the Oilers were staying. I still wasn't activated. Snake came up to me and asked how I was handling Al Davis. I told him, "Your boy's an asshole."

He just grinned. The Oilers were cordial, but they had a game to play. The night before the game, I met Bum and Carl for drinks. Naturally, I'd already had more than a couple of drinks earlier. As I walked out of the lobby bar, I ran into Dale Robertson and I just lashed out. I screamed at him and grabbed him. Another writer from Houston, John McClain, grabbed one arm trying to pull Dale away and I grabbed the other. Dale was getting stretched, screaming, "Goddammit, this is a new leather jacket!"

I chased Dale into the parking lot.

"You're the reason I got run out of town, you jackass."

I never caught him and I thought, "that's real impressive, Dante." I was seething. I sped off, drunk, and had a wreck on the way home. I ran into a tree, banging my nose against the steering wheel and peeling back a chunk of skin that needed 41-stitches. I sat there with blood all over my face, feeling like an ass and all alone. An ambulance took me to the hospital and the police easily could have charged me with DWI, but they didn't.

When we got to New Orleans for the Super Bowl, I was at a bar with a writer for the New York Times when someone recognized me and asked, "What are you?"

I turned toward him and said, "Out of control and dangerous."

The headline in the story the writer did about me said, "Drinking Dan Is Raiders' Sad, Bad Boy."

We beat the Eagles to win the Super Bowl. After all those years working toward it, dreaming about it, cherishing the thought of winning a Super Bowl, I stood on the sideline in New Orleans the entire game half-drunk, wishing I was anywhere but there. I wasn't a part of it. I probably should have been a bigger man than Al Davis. I shouldn't have resorted to the bottle, but it was all I had. I didn't draw a sober breath the whole week I was in New Orleans. I was so alone, not even the guys in the locker-room wanted to be seen talking with me, because Al might find out about it. After the game, I walked up to Plunkett and shook his hand.

"Jimmy I just want to tell you, I'm happy for you. I got injured and you did a great job. I'm glad one of us won the Super Bowl. Congratulations."

He was very short and quick with me, "OK, thanks."

When I got my Super Bowl ring, I gave it away to a charity auction.

CHAPTER FIFTEEN

"I'm not paying you, Pastorini."

All I had to do was pass my physical and it didn't matter what Al Davis said or did, the last three years of my contract would be guaranteed. I would get paid. I busted my ass before training camp in 1981, even though I knew Al never would play me again and would do everything he could to trade me. He hated me and I hated him, it was obvious to everyone in the organization. I knew I would get my chance because there wasn't much of a choice but for Al to play me in the preseason. He couldn't play only Plunkett or Wilson the entire preseason. And I still was on the roster, so I knew even if it was just the preseason, I could show my coaches and teammates–and other teams—just how full of shit Al was the year before.

Two months before training camp opened, I rode in a charity bike-a-thon for City Of Hope in Newport Beach. It was just a fundraiser like so many golf tournaments, tennis tournaments and other events I always enjoyed. They put me on a racing bike and I clipped my feet in. It was an easy ride, but early in the ride as I turned with other cyclists, my front wheel got caught up with someone's bike and I flipped and crashed. I vaulted over the handlebars and landed on my throwing shoulder. It was a third-degree separation and fracture of my collarbone. Once again, I went to Cedars Sinai for surgery and they removed a piece of my right collarbone. While I was recovering at the hospital, I thought, what the hell else can happen? Now I had the shoulder to deal with on top of my ribs and nerve damage. The Raiders placed me on the physically unable to perform list when training camp began, but I busted my ass every day on the field, in the training room, working out. All I wanted and needed for my parents, my daughter and my future, was to pass the physical. Al tried everything to embarrass me. Two weeks into camp, without any notice or time to stretch and loosen up, Al walked up to me and said, "You're throwing today."

I quickly loosened my shoulder and arm as best I could and began throwing routes to Bobby Chandler. I threw darts. With Al and all the coaches watching, I threw tight spirals and they were getting there quick. I threw ins, outs, curls, come-backs, deep-outs. My arm was killing me, like it was on fire from my finger-tips, all the way up my arm and down my ribs, but you never would have known it. I almost bit my tongue, trying to hide the pain. The blank expression on Al's face never changed as I made every throw. He just watched with his arms crossed, then turned to Tom and said, "OK, activate him." And he walked away

I did it. I guaranteed the next three years of my contract. Al was pissed-off and still isolated me from the team, but I didn't give a shit. I went through the rest of the camp still mostly alone, since everybody knew Al was black-balling me. He didn't play me in the first preseason game, or the second, or the third. He waited until the final preseason game to play me, when we played New England. We were down 21-3 when Plunkett came out. As soon as I got into the game, I started picking them apart. I had a hell of a game. I brought us all the way back, threw a couple of touchdowns and gave us a lead, before they took the lead back. I got into the huddle with a big smile on my face on our last drive and said, "Let's go, boys, let's win this thing."

Gene Upshaw looked at me and said, "Look at the kid, trying to win a preseason game."

"Hey, I feel like a kid, Gene. It's been a long time. It's fun to be back."

He told me, "Nice to have you back, man."

I drove us deep into their territory and hit Cliff Branch right in the chest on a crossing route, but the ball popped up and Steve Nelson intercepted the ball. I got to the locker-room still feeling pretty good about how I played. Raymond Chester came up to me and said, "You looked good. You haven't missed a beat."

It didn't matter that I was black-listed, a lot of guys came up and congratulated me. The next day I was stretching on the practice field, when Al Davis came up to me, pointed at me and said, "You're cut."

I was stunned. He waited until the last possible moment, when most NFL rosters already were set, and then he cut me.

"What? Are you shitting me?"

"Nope. You're cut. Get out of here."

I told him, "Well, I'll get you the address where you can send my checks."

"Fuck you," he said. "I'm not paying you, Pastorini."

He waved his hand as if shooing me like a dog, turned and walked away.

As he walked away, I shouted, "We'll see about that, asshole."

I called my agent Tommy and we decided to sue the Raiders and Davis for breach of contract. It was clear what his plan was all along. He kept me around as long as he could. I was one of the highest-paid quarterbacks in football and he was spreading rumors about me. Nobody was going to touch me. He hated my guts because I didn't cower to his ass or kiss his ring. Money had nothing to do with it. The thing that pissed him off the most was he wanted to beat me in a personal war.

After I left Oakland, I just sat on my ass for half the year, trying to figure out how I would make a living and wondering if my career was over, until the Rams finally called. They gave me a separate contract from the deal that would be decided in court. It was for $200,000. I wound up starting a few games, but didn't really play well. The system was completely different than anything I'd played before and it was just a screwed-up fit for me from the start. It was a dysfunctional team. There even was a rumor that Rams owner Georgia Frontierire and I had an affair. My teammates gave me a hard time about it, but nothing was further from the truth. When they fired coach Ray Malavasi at the end of the year, they called me in to tell me they were releasing me, too. I figured I was done. And my money was locked up in court because of Al Davis, so I did what every other out of work person does in Los Angeles. I got into acting. I had been prodded by Hollywood-types to give it a serious try ever since I did Killer Fish. June and Farrah both encouraged me to do it, too. The Playgirl thing was pretty big, so I started taking acting classes with Sal Dano, who was one of Hollywood's best. He was brilliant. He worked with Tom Selleck, Priscilla Barnes, Robert Hays, Catherine Bach. A friend of mine, Tim Rossovich, who played for the Eagles, worked with Sal, too. When I saw myself in Killer Fish, I realized I couldn't act my way out of a paper bag. I was bad. The competitor in me made me want to prove I could act. Sal really pushed all the students and brought the best out of us. I was surrounded by serious actors and serious talent. Sal was one of the best coaches I ever had, in any sport. He got me to put aside all my inhibitions and insecurities. If I didn't do a scene right, he reamed my ass. When he cast me alongside Marta Dubois in Death Of A Salesman, I realized he thought I had a future. Marta already was on her way to becoming a big success and was the best actress I ever knew. She could take a role and do it perfectly—it didn't matter if she played a hooker, a businesswoman, a nun, a mom. Because I was working with Sal, I started getting more work. I did an episode of Fantasy Island, an episode of Voyagers and a bigger role in B.J. and the Bear.

Tim Rossovich's girlfriend was the gatekeeper at the Playboy Mansion, so I wound up there several times and made a bunch of friends and connections with all the Hollywood types. I had been there with June, so Hugh Hefner knew me and I had an open invitation. The thing about the Playboy Mansion was once you were in, you're in, and it wasn't always just about big parties with Playboy Bunnies and stars. It was just a place to go and hang out. At one party at the Mansion, though, I met Vikki Lamotta—Jake Lamotta's wife. She was doing a photo spread for the magazine. She was pretty direct, she and I hit it off and she was flat-out wild in the sack. We wound up shacking up at the mansion for a few days. When I left, I told her, "You can't let any of this get out. I don't want Jake finding me and killing me."

They had been divorced for years, but Jake Lamotta was a crazy man. When the magazine came out, a couple of actors at Sal's school started giving me a hard time and then showed me the magazine article. Vikki was asked in the article about her love interests and the greatest sex she's had. She mentioned me. She talked about me like I was some kind of Italian Stallion or something, and I thought, "Oh, man. I'm going to die."

Another gig I got through Sal was a TV special called Battle of the Las Vegas Showgirls, with Regis Philbin. Showgirls? I told Sal that I was typecast. It was a competition among Las Vegas Showgirls for prizes. Regis and I hosted the show, with Beverly Malden, a beautiful Riviera Hotel girl on the show. Beverly and I hit it off, but she was married and as much as I enjoyed the ladies, I never messed around with married women. The show was fun, except for Regis constantly calling me "Don." I finally told him, "Call me Dan or add a 'tay' to the end of it." He finally got it.

I then did the pilot for a Smokey and the Bandit sequel called "Rooster," with Paul Williams and Pat McCormick. I was getting better as an actor, thanks to Sal. Rooster was a fun set. Pat pretty much drank the whole time we shot. By the end of each day, he would be so drunk he could hardly finish his lines. I was feeling pretty good about how things were going–good enough that I began to think I was over football forever. Then I get a call from Dick Vermeil, asking me to come to Philadelphia. I didn't want to go. I pretty much was downtrodden, tired of football and giving acting a real shot. I even went to rehab for alcohol. What the hell was I going to do in Philly, anyway? Ron Jaworski was there, but Dick called several times, begging me to come out there and talk.

"This is the end for me," I told him.

"I don't believe that, Dan. You've got some football left in you and we've got Sid Gilman running the offense now. It's the same system you ran before and we've simplified it. Just come out here so we can talk."

Vermeil recruited me out of high school when he was an assistant coach at Stanford, so because I respected him I took the visit. He introduced me to everyone in camp and all the guys came up and were real nice. I talked to Jaworski and actually felt awkward, kind of bad for him. I mean, this is the team we beat in the Super Bowl when I was at Oakland and they're bringing me in behind the quarterback that took them there? But Jaws was classy. When I got to Vermeil's office, he slid a contract across the table.

"Fill it out. Put any number you want on it."

I said, "What's up, Dick? Cut to the chase."

"I want you to play for us. I don't like the way you were treated in Oakland. This is going to be a strike year. I won't play you unless all our quarterbacks go down. I want you to be in the system for a year and push Jaworski next year. I want you to make our quarterback position better."

I went back to L.A. with an offer to back-up Jaworski for $200,000. I went to Sal Dano's class and told him, "I think I'm going to go with the Eagles."

"OK," he told me, "but come to class tomorrow."

When I got to Sal's class the next day, he announced, "We're not working today. We're celebrating one of our students moving on."

I was floored. No one ever had given me such a tribute like Sal did.

"When you have opportunities to fly, you fly," Sal told the class. "You have to soar with the eagles. You have to spread your wings and fly with the eagles. Dan will fly with the eagles."

He gave me a Burwood plaque, on top of which was a crystal eagle, with its wings spread, flying. I stood there, stunned. The class was filled with unbelievable actors who were on their way to great things. They all applauded my effort. I couldn't have been more touched.

"When you finish with football," Sal told me, "come back here. You can work in this town."

I signed the two-year deal with the Eagles and, just like Dick said, I never played a down in 1982. I hung around a lot with Sid Gilman, picking up the offense and getting to know Sid again. He had mellowed a lot since 1975. It was good working with him and I had a lot of heart-to-hearts with Dick, too. I think they looked at me as kind of a sage old veteran that could teach guys a lot about persevering through injuries and setbacks. Dick was that kind of guy, kind of a romantic and an emotional man. He wanted every part of the team to be Super Bowl-caliber. The only thing about Dick, though, was he cared more than there were hours in a day. The days he kept were killing him. He spent hours in his office and on the practice field, then had brutally long and meticulous meetings. Sid had long meetings in Houston, but his were nothing compared to Dick's. Dick would go on and on, passionately, even crying sometimes, about the same things, over and over again. I just about fell asleep in my chair several times.

During one ridiculously long meeting, I turned to look at Sid sitting in the corner of the room and he rolled his eyes at me, as if to say, "When's this thing going to end?"

I said, "Hey, asshole, you're the one who taught him this shit."

The next year, Vermeil surprised a lot of people and retired. Even though I knew it would hurt my chances of playing, I was happy he left the game. Dick was killing himself. He cried all the time when he started talking about family and team. He meant every word of it. He was an emotional guy and I liked him. When they brought in Marion Campbell, I never got a chance to compete or play. Campbell brought in Dick Wood as his offensive coordinator and that's when I realized it was time to walk away from the game.

I knew more than the offensive coordinator. There was an offensive blocking scheme that I knew would put Jaworski in a bad spot. I didn't agree with the key for the hot receiver, and I brought it up to Jaworski, hoping he would pick it up and use it. Anytime Wood told Jaworski something wrong, the wrong read or key, I walked up behind Jaworski and told him what the blitz pick-up or read really should be. Wood didn't appreciate me doing that, but I didn't want Jaworski to get killed out there.

Wood never played me, except when the game was out of hand. We were losing to the Cowboys 37-7 late, and he put me in. A few games later, we were losing to the Giants 23-0 late when he put me in. Both times, he called pass plays with nobody in the backfield to help with pass blocking. He was trying to get me crushed. When I realized what he was doing against the Cowboys, I ignored his play, called maximum-protection in the huddle and threw the ball away. I threw one pass over everybody, one pass into the bench and one pass out of bounds. He called three-straight pass plays with no protection, at the point in the game when guys on the other side were trying to pile up sack stats. I wasn't stupid. I saw what he was doing. Before the third pass play, Cowboys linebacker D.D. Lewis shouted at me, "Hey, Pasto, you gonna throw it away again?"

"Yep."

After the Cowboys game, I confronted Wood.

"Don't ever do that to me again. If you want to see what I can do, put me in the game when it's 0-0 and let me call my own plays. If you do it again, I'm going to do the same damn thing."

And he did it again when we faced Lawrence Taylor and the Giants. He told Marion Campbell to put me in late and then called back-to-back pass plays with no back to protect me. I didn't even look around for receivers. I just took a three-step drop and threw it over everybody.

The rest of the year, I just played out the string, eventually dating Beverly after she left her husband. I played in a lot of charity golf and tennis events, trying to map out my future, looking for work. After the season I was at a charity golf tournament with a business owner that I asked to hire me as a marketing guy, someone who had name-recognition and a little hustle that could help his company. We sat around drinking Black Sambuca, getting drunk, when he said, "I'd love to play Augusta, but I don't think I ever will."

"So why don't you, you've got money?" I asked.

"I can't get on Augusta National. Some things money can't buy."

I bet him that I could get him on the course and he told me he'd already tried every way he knew and the Members just didn't allow it very often.

Then, he told me, "Dan, I'll bet you $10,000 against one dollar that you couldn't get onto Augusta within six months."

I took the bet. Two weeks later, I called him and said, "I got you on."

I called a guy, who called a guy, who knew PGA commissioner Deane Bemon. An Augusta National member said he could get us on for one day if we gave him $6,000. A week later, I got picked up in a private jet in Philadelphia and we flew to Georgia. We got there bright and early, played 18 holes, broke for lunch, played another 18, then played the Par 3 course. We got dressed for dinner and Beman joined us, as we ate an amazing dinner and drank $300 bottles of Chateau Lafitte Rothschild. The golf was $6,000, dinner came to about $5,000 and on the plane back to Philadelphia my buddy said, "You're amazing, Pastorini," and handed me a check for $10,000. The only bad part was, the guy didn't hire me.

Beverly and I gradually began a serious relationship and once again I fell in love. We got married in a great ceremony in Steamboat Springs, Colo. and bought a house there. The place was perfect, the marriage was perfect. I loved to ski. I loved the outdoors. I hunted, I fished.

By the time summer rolled around, I still wasn't sure if football was out of my system. Bum was fired from Houston after the 1980 season and was coaching in New Orleans, when he invited me to the Saints' 1984 mini-camp. I did well enough that he invited me to Vero Beach, Fla. for training camp. I packed my bags and was about to walk out of the house when the telephone rang. It was the media relations guy from the Saints.

He said, "Well, other than that how'd you like the play, Mrs. Lincoln?"

"What do you mean?"

He handed the phone to Bum and Bum told me he couldn't bring me to camp. He said that with Ken Stabler and Richard Todd on the roster, he couldn't justify to the owner, John Mecom, adding another high-priced quarterback.

"Whoa, whoa, wait a minute, Bum. I'm not under contract. I'm coming to try out and if I'm good enough to make your football team, then we'll talk money. All I want is a chance. Let me compete."

He told me, "I can't do it, Dan"

That was the last dagger in the heart. When Bum told me I couldn't play anymore, that was it.

CHAPTER SIXTEEN

Quarterback Sneak

I hung up the phone and stared out my window at the mountains. There was no lonelier feeling than my NFL career coming to an end. It rarely happens on the players' terms and I was no different. I got a phone call. That's it. I was done. I knew it was coming, but unlike the real world I could never say the exact day that I planned to retire. There was no build-up or chance to wrap my mind around the idea of retirement. There was no gold watch, no press conference, no teary farewell. It just slapped me in the face. That's it.

Money was bad, too. I thought about a lot of things staring at those Rocky Mountains, like why the hell I married Beverly. We already both realized it was a mistake. I tried to keep paying mom and dad, hoping to keep them OK, but that had to stop. I called dad.

"I can't do it anymore, dad. I'm sorry."

He said he understood, thanked me and said he wanted to start looking for more work again, anyway, but I felt everything falling in on me like a flood. My contract was tied up in court because of Al Davis and I got slapped with the harsh reality of getting turned out into the world with no money and no way to make a living. I didn't take Sal up on his promise to get me work if I went back to his acting school. I went back to my first love.

I never lost my passion for racing. I thought with that passion, my hustle marketing and making contact with sponsors, with some luck I could carve out a nice living. The only thing I had was my name and the best way I could still capitalize on it was a career in racing. I was experienced, I'd raced, gone to driving schools and knew a lot of people in the industry. I called Bobby Rowe, who was my former drag-boat crew chief, who worked in Memphis.

"Let's go racing, Bobby," I told him. "Let's figure this out."

We had talked about it over the years, sometimes as just a pipe dream and sometimes seriously, until Bum put in my '78 contract that I couldn't race. We called Frank Taylor, an interesting and a passionate racing guy we knew in California. Frank had a Top Fuel dragster named Dago Red that was for sale. I knew Dago Red was too small for me to fit into, but if I got that car I could then sell it and get a bigger one. Besides, the best part of the deal was getting his racing operation, which was the truck, tools, car, spare parts, motors, everything. I took out a second mortgage on my house in Steamboat, negotiated the deal with Frank, left Beverly and went to Pomona to take delivery on the car.

It was cheaper for me to enter the race and get my crew into Pomona for three days than buying tickets and pit passes for everybody, so that's what I did. I entered that race with no intention of racing. We just needed to be at the track to take inventory and go over everything in the operation. We had the car in the pits working every day, working on the motor, greasing parts, cleaning. On the last day of racing, a couple of guys who had been in the pits next to us all weekend came up to us, crossed their arms and one said, "We're just curious. We noticed you guys work harder than anybody out here, but you never race the car. What's the deal?"

It was Manny Asadurian and Lee Donabedian, a couple of Armenian boys. I laughed, told them my story and they invited us over to their bus to hang out. I instantly became friends with Manny and Lee that day. But that's just how it is in racing, everyone helps each other, unlike football when everyone seems to be out to get you. There's a lot of, "bench racing" that goes on, guys sitting together on benches after the race day, bullshitting and telling race stories.

Bobby and I drove the rig to Memphis and I helped Bobby with his shop, while I tried to find a sponsor, another car and book Match Races all over the country. I was chief cook and bottle-washer on that team. In the NFL, everything you ever need is given to you. You need some pills? Here, take 'em. You need money while you're on the road? Here, here's your per diem. You need medical attention, equipment, clothes, gear? You want dinner? You want to watch a movie? Here, here, here. On the racing circuit, you're not given a damn thing and I loved it. I had my hands on every little detail with the team, from ordering T-shirts, to booking races and helping in the garage. I knew match races would be a good place for me to advance up the NHRA circuit, because I could put people in the stands and if I got lucky, win a few races, make the NHRA nationals tour, and get on network TV, which gets the attention of sponsors.

We had everything but a car that fit. I made calls all over the circuit and heard Gene Snow was selling his car, because he wanted to go to a shorter wheel base. We wound up selling our car to Eddie Hill and I bought Gene Snow's. The only thing left to do was get my NHRA license. We took delivery of the car and trailered it to Green Valley Raceway in Dallas for our licensing runs.

The first time I drove the car was after I invested all the money I had, put the team together, promised race promoters I would race and took care of all the details on the team. I got into the car and hit it to burn out the tires. It got my attention. When it came to the sensation of speed, drag-racing a boat 130-mph was supposed to be the same as racing a car 270-mph, but as I sat there, I realized that was a lie. The power was amazing on the burnout. I backed up and the moment of truth finally arrived.

My crew chief told me, "Mash it and get off it."

So I mashed that thing and it almost knocked me out, because of the G-force. I was sitting with my head forward. It was like, warp-speed six, Scotty. Streaks of light flew past me and I thought, oh, man, I may have bitten off more than I can chew. The first few passes I did going full-track were mind-boggling. They also were the greatest rush I ever felt driving. I just loved the speed more than I ever thought.

When I got to NHRA licensing, I did a couple of burnouts and then what we called a "squirt"–just a short, loud little launch. Then they asked me to do a burnout, a backup and a squirt. Then they asked me to do a burnout, a backup and a half-track pass. I did that three times for the officials judging my qualifying, then they asked me to do a three-quarter track pass. In order to qualify, the last thing I had to do was a full-pass within a certain few tenths of a second of the world record. Gene Snow actually signed off on my credentials because on one of my full-pass runs my parachute didn't open, but I still managed to stop the car.

That showed I could handle the car. I had my license, now we could race.

I named my car, "Quarterback Sneak" and hustled sponsors, but I knew until I got on TV, my only source of funding would have to be from match races. I knew everything there was to know about match races and I knew all the Top Fuel drivers, from my days in Sonora reading racing magazines, to the match-races I did in college in my '67 Chevelle. Match races were the lifeblood of the drag-racing industry. There was Billy "The Waco Kid" Myer, Raymond Beadle and the Blue Max, the Budweiser King, Kenny Bernstein, Don "The Snake" Prudhomme, Tom "The Mongoose" McKewen. They were all like characters out of a superhero book, on Hot Wheels toys, that had great followings and capitalized on their personalities. Tracks all over the world wanted the big names and they would pay good money for them to show up for match races. That's where I figured I could pay a few bills. If I went to a match race, I could race, sell some t-shirts, make $15,000 or so and then put what I could together to get into the NHRA races. If I established myself, I could earn $20,000 to $25,000 racing another big-name drag racing star.

My first race was in March of 1985 at Bakersfield, Calif. It was the largest non-sanctioned race in the world. There were two separate fields of 16 and I had big plans of making a big splash. Instead, I was eliminated in the first-round, because when I saw the yellow light flash, I waited for the tree to turn green.

When I stopped at the end of the run, my crew chief Bobby Rowe, who raced Funny Cars, told me, "Uh, Dan, you may want to leave on yellow. It takes four-tenths of a second for that to register in your mind and go down to your throttle foot to mash. As soon as you see yellow, go."

"OK, lesson learned," I told him, laughing.

I packed in the crowd at Alamo Dragway in San Antonio to race Chris Karamecines, The Greek. Chris was a great guy and there was a lot of media out to see me race, too. That's when I struck a deal with Linda Vaughn, the famous Miss Hurst Golden Shifter, who became a great asset helping me get more exposure. Linda knew everyone in racing and was one of the most popular people on the circuit. She was leggy, busty and voluptuous. My kinda girl. She absolutely stole the show everywhere she went, with her tight skirts, low-cut blouses and go-go boots. But she was a legitimate marketing genius and helped us get some credibility. She knew everybody and opened a lot of doors for me. On the track I had to prove myself just like everyone else, but track owners noticed quickly that it would pay off bringing me in to race. We packed the stands everywhere we went and I showed I could drive, too. Tracks and races got a lot of publicity because I was a novelty for the newspapers and TV stations. I did every interview anyone asked, then worked on the car, raced, sold t-shirts and signed autographs. Everywhere we went, if there was a story in a newspaper or magazine, we'd cut out the articles, put them in scrapbooks and make copies to send to other track owners. I tracked how many minutes of air time I got on TV and on the radio and bundled those numbers along with pictures in my proposals to track owners and sponsors. I did it all out of necessity and passion for what I did, but I started putting together some pretty, good proposals. I convinced everyone on the circuit that I wasn't a novelty and this wasn't a pastime for me, but a business that I took very seriously.

We tested a Waterman Injector System in Gainesville in September of 1985, in a race against Bill Mullins. When I mashed the pedal, the car took off like a rocket. When the car hit 1,000-feet, I heard a big gasp of air. It pushed me forward in the car and the car swerved hard to the left. Everything was happening very fast and I heard the oil pan scraping the ground. One of the first things I learned in racing was that if there ever was trouble, pull the chute immediately. It was branded on my brain: Pull the parachute, pull the chute. As I headed into the next lane, I pulled the chute and it straightened out the car. It snapped me back in a line, but the brakes didn't work because both rear tires blew off the car. The motor burst into a ball of flames and everybody in the stands gasped, but as I stopped the car all I thought was, "There goes fifty grand for an engine."

Something else I learned early-on, if you race, you're going to have an accident. You just have to handle it. My family actually was supportive and knew I felt safer racing. My mom was impressed that I turned into an enterprising businessman, with the t-shirt sales, building the team and starting my racing business. We just went week-to-week trying to build the team.

When we didn't have a good showing in Baton Rouge, I wound up splitting with Bobby and getting Donnie Couch for the 1986 season as my crew chief. In Memphis, we didn't have a garage, just a bay at the end of one of his friends' body shop. There was a lot of partying going on instead of business and I told Bobby one day, "We're not doing this right. I'm trying to run a business and make money."

I moved everything to Houston and Donnie Couch and I went to Gainesville, Fla. for our first race together. In the first round, I beat the great Shirley Muldowney on a hole-shot, beating her off the line and to the finish line, even though she had a faster time line-to-line. I always was quick off the line. It was my first win in a national competition in the Quarterback Sneak. Donnie worked for a lot of different teams and when he joined us, we started running a lot better and faster. Our entire team was Donnie, our truck driver and me. I paid bills, bought parts and fuel and made reservations in hotels. I packed chutes, put air in the tires, mixed Nitro, pulled the heads off the motor and helped Donnie work on it. Donnie drove the car hauler from race-to-race and I flew, so I could book races, search for sponsors, do promotions and pay bills.

We lost to "Big Daddy" Don Garlits in the semi-finals in Gainesville, but I was with him off the line and we were side-by-side at 1,000 feet, before he left me behind. Garlits became the first driver to break the 270-mph barrier in that race. I lost, but it was the fastest side-by-side race in drag-racing history. People didn't take us lightly anymore. Next up was Columbus, Ga. And I couldn't have felt better, or worse. I finally had the car running the way I wanted it to run and proved myself against Shirley Muldowney and Big Daddy. The NHRA loved the publicity and took us as a serious threat. But I was out of money. The race in Gainesville tapped me out.

Larry Enderli, my friend from Baytown, Tx. that Jim Franciscus and I spent July Fourth Weekend with in 1979, saved me. After Gainesville, I was at Larry's house and told him, "I just can't do it anymore. I don't have enough to survive."

"I've got a funny feeling that you're going to make it," he told me. "Go to Columbus and see what you can do. We'll talk about the future when you get back."

Larry gave me money to keep the team going for another week. Only Donnie and I went to Columbus, hiring a makeshift crew of guys from the track to chip in and help us. I won my first-round race over Dick Lahaie. Then I beat Gary Beck. The track was not ideal, everyone had to pedal—in other words, catch a pause in the track, shift and keep going. It wasn't an easy thing to do at those speeds, but it's something I learned. I kept winning and finally made it to the final round against Gene Snow. My car was a mess, though. I had tires that were worn out, so Raymond Beadle, my friend from Blue Max, lent me two tires. I had two burned pistons and, remarkably, Gene Snow, the guy I bought the car from and I was about to race in the final, gave me two pistons. That's why I loved drag racing. That's how the circuit was. Gene helped out a fellow driver, because he wanted to beat me fair and square. As we got the car ready for my first championship final, the Pro Stock cars ran, then the Funny Cars and then it started to rain. The final was postponed to the next day.

For me, it meant more expenses because of another night in Columbus, but when we got up the next morning, it was a beautiful, sunbird day. The day before, 10,000 people were in the stands. When I lined up to face Snow, there were about ten. I lined up against Gene Snow and beat him. It was like winning a playoff game. I was speechless. The week before, I considered selling everything and ending my racing career. Overnight, I was a winner on the NHRA circuit and had credibility as a serious racer in the series.

CHAPTER SEVENTEEN

"I would have shot Mr. Pastorini"

Not long after my first win, I went to Denver to meet a vice-president for marketing of the Coors Brewing Company. My win made national headlines, not just in racing circles, but on newscasts, sports shows and in newspapers all over the country. Kenny Youngblood did a rendering of my dragster emblazoned with the Coors Light logo. I practiced my presentation as if it were a playoff gameplan. I memorized it and thought about all the questions that might be asked and how I would answer them. I had scrapbooks of all the stories written about me in newspapers and magazines. I had data on how much time I had been interviewed on local and national television. I had statistics on how many more fans showed up at tracks when I raced. I sat there nervously when I got to the Coors headquarters, then the door opened and the brand manager walked in. He had a look on his face like he could give a damn who I was or what I was doing. He was small and looked like Mr. Peepers. I thought, "This isn't going to end well."

I gave the presentation as if it were a waste of my time and his. I just half-assed my way through it. When I finished, I started packing my things and was about to stand up and thank him for his time, when he said, "I like it. Let's do it." He turned to Steve Saunders, who was in charge of racing sponsorship, and told Steve to get me on the team. Coors Light sponsored me for $350,000 for three years. The ideal amount would have been twice as much in order to reach the elite level, but I wasn't in a position to haggle. I wasn't complaining. I became a legitimate fixture on the NHRA Top Fuel circuit less than two years after I finished my football career. We raced under the Coors banner and had a very good year, finishing seventh overall in points.

We bought a new car for '87 and I had new crew chief, Jimmy Brisette, who joined me when Donnie moved out on his own. Brisette did a good job, but the new car was inconsistent. When we raced in Indianapolis, we blew out rods on three engines on consecutive runs. That's $75,000 a pop. We couldn't afford to keep doing that, so we got back to Houston and took apart the car, head to toe. We figured out a problem in the fuel cell caused the hesitation, but it cost us a lot of time and money before we got the car running right. We were in danger of losing the Coors Light sponsorship and running out of money. That's how fragile racing can be. We had a bad fuel cell that kept us out of the points race, and Coors Light shuffled their management team.

Before I went to Columbus, Ohio, I had a match race in Seattle. The tractor trailer pulling my car hauler got overheated and the heads on the engine broke. I had to get to Columbus just to survive and keep the team alive–I was just about out of money. I went to a truck dealer, begging for sympathy and a new tractor-trailer, so I could pull the car-hauler to Ohio.

"I don't have good credit. I'm busted. But I need to get to Columbus."

The dealer knocked $10,000 off the price, somehow approved my loan and I hit the road to Columbus on Wednesday afternoon. Qualifying for the race was Thursday and Friday, but I phoned ahead and told the race organizers my predicament. I pulled into Columbus at 3 a.m. Saturday morning and got about two hours sleep, as my crew prepared the car in the parking lot. I had one shot to qualify for the race and when I got that chance, I qualified on my one-and-only shot. I qualified ninth. That was the good news. The bad news was I had to face the No. 1 qualifier, "Big Daddy" Don Garlits.

Somehow, I beat the legend. The fans went nuts. Beating Big Daddy was no small feat. He had all the best technology, crew and sponsorships. I told reporters that Big Daddy could make a bathtub go 270-mph. When I beat him, the crowd reaction was bedlam, like the return to the Astrodome in '78 but on a smaller scale. Fans jumped up and down on the bleachers, waved, and I waved back. I beat him on a hole-shot and he was pissed off. After we crossed the line, he drove his car all the way down the turn aisle, toward his trailer and onto his trailer. He got out, threw his stuff into the trailer, backed out his rig and drove off the property. Oh, man, was it an unbelievable win. A lot of people thought I was crazy for entering racing so late in the game, but people I raced against understood the rush that fueled me. It's a phenomenal thing when you go out and take a car to its maximum capability and control it.

Fans related to me and they were fantastic. I always made sure to interact with fans, not just for the sake of the sponsorship, but because they were the most loyal fans of any sport. I just loved race fans. Win, lose or draw, if they loved you they loved you forever. As long as you were out there and you were their guy, they backed you. When you lost, they didn't get pissed-off, boo you or vandalize your house and car. They mourned with you. It was the total opposite of what I experienced in football. Racing fans were the best fans in the world, period. Auto racing media was great with me, too. I always told them that if I could have made a living racing, I might not ever have stepped on a football field. I loved the racing and the interaction. Before that race against Big Daddy in Ohio, I was working on my dragster and couldn't find a wrench. One of my hands was on the motor and I reached out with my other hand when I heard someone say, "Here ya go." I thought it was a member of the crew, but it was a fan standing in our pits. I tightened the bolt, looked up, shook his hand and told him, "We must be fine, there aren't any parts left over."

That's just how it was everywhere we went. My team was voted "Fan Favorite" at the end of the year and we were feeling pretty good. The car was running great, I had a girlfriend, a great girl named Dena Kindred in Houston, and an appeals court sided with me in my lawsuit against Al Davis. I was rewarded the $450,000 I was owed. Judge Betty Barry-Deal said, "The contract guaranteed Pastorini's salary even if his skill or performance was unsatisfactory." Al Davis still refused to pay me and took it to a higher court, but I thought it would be only a matter of time before he would be forced to pay me.

The last thing I wanted after two failed marriages was a serious girlfriend. I told the auto racing media that the Coors Light dragster was my lady. But I met Dena through Karen Henry, who was Tommy Vance's assistant and had a boutique P.R. company. Dena was an aerobics instructor that owned the Bodyworks salon in Houston. Dena loved the social limelight, which I always could provide, for better and worse. Dena and I quickly became an item in the gossip and society columns, since I always took part in charity events, galas, golf tournaments or whatever the event might be.

I finally got the call I suspected I would get. One of the marketing guys at Coors called me and said, "Racing is not in our demographic."

I told him, "You don't like guys who go to the races and drink beer?"

I couldn't figure that one out. I had become one of the most popular drivers in the NHRA. Attendance at NHRA events went up. Even Coors Light profits went up when I raced. I didn't take credit for that, but whatever we were doing was working. We stated our case to Coors Light, but they weren't just dropping me, they dropped Tom McEwon with the Coors Mongoose and also Bill Elliott, who drove the Coors car in NASCAR. The bottom line was I needed to win. If you're not winning, you're not going to get sponsors, it doesn't matter what your name is.

I ran a special Top Fuel challenge race in Dallas and ran pretty well, finishing second. When I got back to Houston, Dena had a surprise party for me, a kind of victory party at Armando's. Dena and I definitely partied. By the end of the night, I was in no condition to drive, so I told Dena I would shift the stick on my Porsche if she drove. We went off down the road, Dena pushing the clutch and me shifting. I told her to punch it and, sure enough, we saw police lights flash on behind us, so we exited and pulled over. It was just a bad vibe from the start when the officers came up to the car. It was a brand-new Porsche, so the paper tags on the back of the car had my name printed on it. One officer asked Dena to get out of the car, lowered his head to look at me in the passenger seat and said, "Hello, Mr. Pastorini."

I sat there, and sat there . . . and sat there, as they spoke to Dena behind the car. I sat there for at least 15-minutes, until I finally got out, realizing Dena may have had too much to drink and was in trouble. I asked the officer, "I'd like to know if you're arresting her, so I could call someone to come get the car. I'm in no condition to drive."

The officer told me to get back in the car. I asked again if I could call someone. Two other officers who had showed up came toward me. All I wanted was to make sure my new car would be taken care-of, but they seemed hell-bent on getting a reaction out of me. They all knew who I was and I found myself staring at some of those officers you hear about—on a power trip, or some kind of mission to put a celebrity in his place.

"I need to make some plans here!"

One officer told me to get back in the car and shoved me across the chest with his billy club. I pushed him back and said, "Hey, mother-fucker, keep your hands off me."

He clubbed me on the side of the head, pushed me to the ground and buried my face in the pavement.

They arrested me, threw me in the back of the police car and one of the officers said, "You're going to jail, smart ass."

He seemed to get pleasure out of arresting me, hitting me and throwing me around. I completely lost it in the back of the police car. I totally snapped. I started calling him every name in the book. I screamed at him, kicked the windows and doors of the police car. I told him, "You enjoy fucking with people, mother fucker? Take these cuffs off me and let's settle this just you and me."

I leaned back, put my head on the floor of the back seat and tried to kick out the rear-window. They dragged me out of the car, pushed me into the gravel on the side of the road again and roughed me up, then threw me back into the back of the car.

"You're going to jail, Mr. Football."

The next day, every news story, every newscast started with, "Dan Pastorini was arrested." And in every story, the officer that seemed to have it in for me the most, C.W. Grant, said I called him a nigger. And I did. I called him every word in the book. I lost control. My temper got the best of me because he baited me. Racist was the last thing I ever was and all my friends, former teammates, everyone, knew that. A couple of days after I posted bail, Jerry Levias called me and jokingly said, "Now, Dante, why are you using that word?"

"Jerry, you know me. I'm not that way, you know it. That guy had it in for me from the start, like he got off on getting me to lose it. If anyone was a racist, it was that guy."

George Webster, my old roommate and best man at my wedding with June, called, too. I told him the same thing and he responded the same. George said he would support me any way he could, just like Levias.

But that was the end of Coors Light. So much for the sponsorship.

I was charged with misdemeanor assault and public intoxication. Dena was charged with Driving While Intoxicated and she hired Lewis Dickson and Dick Deguerin as her attorneys. Dena's trial was first and when I testified in it, the three HPD officers were there and Dickson quickly realized they could not corroborate their story. Dickson finally questioned the officer that hit me–C.W. Grant—and he rambled for several minutes, recalling what happened between us.

Dickson asked Grant, "That's when you say Mr. Pastorini called you a nigger?"

"Yes."

The cop just kept babbling about how unruly I was and how much I acted like a racist, and then offered up all on his own, "If it were under different circumstances, I would have shot Mr. Pastorini."

When the judge heard that, a look of shock came across his face, he tossed his pencil into the air and he said, "Mistrial."

The next day was my trial for public intoxication. We got into court 100-percent ready, ready to prove their stories didn't jibe. When the judge walked in, the D.A. stood up and said, "Your honor, we'd like to throw out all charges against Mr. Pastorini."

I guess they didn't want an HPD officer's testimony that he would shoot me to become public record. The next day on the back page of the newspaper in agate type, there was a small story, "Charges dropped against NFL quarterback."

I was facing a crossroads with my race team, but just figured it would all work out. Besides, Dena was doing well. We surprised our friends at a party we had at Dena's penthouse. We invited about 40 people over and when they all arrived, we announced, "Welcome to our wedding" and we all went downstairs to some limousines that were waiting and decked out, complete with Dom Perignon. We drove to the Transco Tower skyscraper and had our wedding in front of a beautiful Water Wall. Then, we had a reception and dinner at Pino's, an exclusive restaurant.

CHAPTER EIGHTEEN

One Dollar

Less than six-months after I got married, I was out of money and out of options with my racing team. I sold everything–the car, tools, trailer, everything. One minute I was that close to breaking through and the next I was out of racing and broke. Al Davis still refused to pay me the money he owed. I called my accountant and asked about my options. I was embarrassed, upset, searching for ways to make a living again. My accountant went through all my finances and it was bleak. He did ask me about a stock I purchased 17-years earlier.

"Did you know about this?" he asked me.

It was the $2,500 I gave Marty Sammons my second year in the league, the money I gave him just so he would quit bugging me. Marty invested it into a stock that split six times and was worth $65,000. I was stunned. I figured that money disappeared like all the investments I made. That $65,000 saved my ass, although it only caught me up on some bills and back taxes I owed the I.R.S. The whole time I struggled keeping the racing team alive, I wasn't paying my taxes like I should have. I always took care of mom and dad and paid June as much child support as I could, before I paid the government. My accountant told me my only option was to file for bankruptcy, so I did.

A few weeks later, I stood outside a building in downtown Houston, tears welling up in my eyes. I told myself that I wasn't owed a damn thing because of my name, so I swallowed my pride and walked into the unemployment office. Standing in the unemployment line, a couple of people asked me for my autograph. I could feel people in the room and behind the counter looking at me. I heard them whispering, but what else could I do?

I got away as I tried to figure things out, driving to Sonora to see mom and dad. I kept as much of my personal financial troubles from them as I could, but parents know. Standing in our kitchen talking to mom one day, she reached into her pocket and handed me the dollar bill that I signed for her at the restaurant when I was a kid.

"Keep that dollar with you always," she told me. It was her way of telling me she knew what was going on and money didn't matter. Money comes and goes. She just wanted me to find happiness. It got bad over the next several months, but no matter how broke I was, I never spent that dollar. I tried to keep my racing career alive, driving Top Fuel dragsters briefly for John Carey and Larry Frazier, making whatever money I could at appearances and autograph shows, setting up meetings with potential investors in a racing operation. I tested at the Daytona International Speedway to join the IMSA Camel GT circuit with Tim McAdam and Chip Mead. I got to the point where I had nothing, absolutely nothing, and searched for any way possible to find a career. I didn't have a job, a car, nothing. But I had that one dollar.

I sat with dad in the family room at his house in San Jose one afternoon and I don't know what made me finally confront him about something that bothered me my entire life. It was the weight of my troubles, probably, or maybe I just broke through one of the walls I always put up.

"Dad, I have to ask you something."

"Sure, Willie, what do you want?"

"How come you never told me you loved me?"

Dad forced a little laugh and squirmed in his chair.

"I gave you so much, Willie. Your mother and I did everything we could for you."

"No, no, no, dad. That's not what I'm asking. I know you love me. But why couldn't you ever tell me you love me? Don't you realize why I accomplished everything in my life? It was because I wanted your approval."

He said, "I always approved. I always was proud."

I just kept pushing him about why he never told me he loved me. I knew he loved me, but why didn't he ever say it? I knew we were ungrateful kids. I knew he never missed one of my games. He never missed a football game, even if it was 120-miles away. He went to two or three baseball games in a week sometimes. Mom held together the restaurant and then dad would work all night. But why didn't he ever say it?

I just kept pressing. He was unnerved and then angry. He stood up as if he was going to walk away, but I stood up and cut him off.

"Why couldn't you, dad? Why couldn't you ever tell me you loved me? Was it me, dad?"

He bowed his head and burst into tears, his shoulders shaking he cried so hard.

"Because nobody ever told me!"

Dad fell into my arms and I hugged him. He raised his head and said, "I love you, Willie. I love you and I'm so proud of you."

Dad told me he loved me every time we spoke after that. We talked more often on the phone and every time, before he hung up he said, "I love you, Willie."

"Call me collect, Willie, call me collect," he told me. "Don't spend that dollar your mother gave you. Call me."

Dena and I moved to Vail, where she got into local TV and teaching aerobics, I got a job with Seagram's, doing events as a spokesperson and had a chance to partner with a restaurant development. I met Sam Shalala in 1992, through Tim McAdam, the IMSA car owner, in Vail. Sam had a Porsche 911 and asked me to race with him.

I had done some road-racing before, did the Bondurant Racing School and tested at Daytona. Next thing I knew, I was a driver in the 24 Hours Of Daytona. Two hours into the 24 Hours, our first driver came into the pits with a broken valve.

Sam said, "Well, I guess that's it."

"Wait a second," I told him. "Do you have a valve and a rocker Why don't we just fix it? That's what we do between rounds in drag-racing"

We hustled together a fix, I went out and raced on five cylinders and we wound up finishing fifth in our class. We beat our car to death. It looked as if it was held together with tape. We ripped it up, banged it, fixed the motor. All of us sat on the pit wall after the race, exhausted and savoring our good finish, with the dirty, beat-up car sitting still in front of us when the driver's side mirror just fell off. All by itself, it just fell to the ground and the mirror broke, like something out of a movie. We busted out laughing.

We all forged a great bond with Bill Sargis, who was a developer out of Maryland and came to the 12 Hours of Sebring with a friend to drive with Sam and I in the race. On the first night of racing, Bill's friend lost his brakes coming out of Turn Three, crashed and died. Bill was devastated, despondent and I just talked with him as much as I could about his friend. Bill went through some hard times after his friend died and eventually moved to Vail, where he wanted to explore investment opportunities. We took over a restaurant at a resort called Pines Lodge that was in receivership and called it Pastorini's.

I was back in the family business, but never got to share the experience with dad. Before we moved to Vail, I got a call from home. Dad went to play golf with his friends, as he always did. He put on his golf shoes, took off in the golf cart to start his round, then realized he didn't strap his bag onto the cart. When he leaned over to pick up the bag, he had a massive heart attack and fell face-first into the ground. He died on the spot.

We dressed dad in his favorite suit for the funeral and he looked great, peaceful, in the casket. Just before they closed the casket, I took the dollar bill I signed and mom gave me, folded it, and put it in dad's coat pocket. I leaned over and told him, "Now you call me anytime, dad," and they closed the casket.

I saw my sister Dorothy and brother-in-law Stan at dad's funeral. Dorothy walked up to me and said, "How you doing?"

"Please get away from me."

A good Christian man should forgive. But I couldn't do it.

At mom and dad's house after the funeral, I was in the kitchen with Butch, just standing there quietly. Butch grabbed one of dad's precious knives that he loved so much and kept so sharp. Butch started scratching the grout between the tiles on the kitchen counter, back and forth, blunting the knife. I shook my head, laughed, and picked up another of dad's knives and started doing the same thing. We blunted every one of dad's knives, laughing and crying at the same time. We just relieved pressure and sort of paid tribute to dad in our own way.

"I'll show you, dad," Butch said. "Who's laughing now about your knives?"

My whole life, I always had to find ways to convince myself that things may have been bad, my life might be a mess, but it wasn't as bad as I thought.

Not quite a year after dad died, the resort pulled the rug out from under us and put their own people in charge of our restaurant, hoping to capitalize on the success Bill and I had built. The restaurant got great reviews in the Denver papers and did quite well, but they didn't allow us to extend our contract. Except for the work I did for Seagram's I had another great investment backfire and was back looking for work.

A lot of things were catching up with me and I really wasn't happy with Dena. I had a pile of I.R.S. bills I couldn't even begin to pay. I felt like a bum not paying my debt and kept trying to catch up, selling everything I could, doing card shows and as much work as I could for Seagram's. I had two images—the one everyone had of me and the one in the mirror. I was just trying to survive, living paycheck to paycheck. But if I was out at a charity event or golf tournament, I was the life of the party. I was the one everybody wanted to talk with and get to know. They wanted to hear my stories and drink with me. I signed autographs and had so many people offer me great business propositions, which usually wound up meaning they wanted money from me. I didn't have money. The more I was surrounded by people who wanted to be with me, the more I realized I was alone.

I didn't have teammates or a racing team to pick me up anymore. My team was me. Carl and Bum worried about me and knew I was battling, but I didn't want those guys to know how bad it was, because of pride. To me, telling someone you needed help would have been a sign of weakness. I couldn't go there. I couldn't admit I was a failure. I wasn't supposed to be a failure.

I filed for my second bankruptcy, looked for work, still chased the racing dream and retreated from my friends and family. June called me in the spring of 1993 and asked if she should talk with the TV newsmagazine A Current Affair. They contacted June and said they wanted to do a story about Brahna and her tennis. June said they would be contacting me, too.

I told her, sure. Brahna definitely got her daddy's right arm and ability to play hurt, as well as my temper. I always kept up with Brahna and her tennis successes through June, but my biggest regret as a person was not being there more for Brahna. It was all my fault and I knew it. I never was sure why I ran away from the best thing I ever accomplished in my life, searching for success in places that didn't matter–bars, business deals, sports, with women. I never saw Brahna from just after her first birthday until she was about 8-years-old. After that, I only saw her off-and-on and talked with her on the phone only occasionally.

Brahna was a fantastic tennis player in high school. She had a big serve with that right arm and from her sophomore year until the end of her senior year, Brahna was undefeated in her matches, going 41-0. She also was incredibly competitive, slamming her racquet into her leg or on the court when she missed a shot and once throwing it across the net. Her senior season, Brahna sprained her ankle badly at the city sectional championship and her coach asked Brahna to forfeit the match. But Brahna was mad, because she was injured and because her opponent laughed at her. She iced her ankle for 10-minutes, taped it and beat the girl 6-1, 6-1, but in the championship the pain was too much and Brahna finally lost. Brahna had an inner-hurt and I was the reason why. Everyone asked about her celebrity mother and father, and I made headlines everywhere, but she didn't see a lot of me.

I saw the Current Affair cameras when I pulled into my driveway one afternoon in Vail. When I got out of my car, a reporter stuck a microphone in my face and said, "Your daughter says you never were around and you didn't pay child support. You daughter says you are a deadbeat dad."

"Whoa, let's go inside and talk about this," I told him.

I told them, "My daughter has a lot of reasons to be angry at me. I didn't run away from my responsibilities, I just couldn't do it. That's not an excuse for not being there for her. June is a good mother and is taking care of her. Brahna's heard things not favorable about me and I'm sure she does have animosity for me. I've done the best I could, when I could. These are not easy times for me right now. A lot of things have happened that people don't know about."

They showed video of Brahna talking about me. She said, "My mother didn't want me growing up hating my father, but I didn't even know who my father was. Dan Pastorini was just a name to me. If I saw him walking down the street, I couldn't even pick him out."

That ripped out my guts. It was the worst hurt I'd ever felt, but I understood why Brahna felt like she did. Anything I could give Brahna, I always gave her. But I was an absentee father. I brought her for visits to Houston. I went to her tennis matches when I was in California. I helped with her tennis lessons. But I understood why she felt the way she felt and that's what hurt the most.

When Brahna graduated, I got the invitation one day before the ceremony. That's when I knew she didn't really want me around and I sunk to another low. I sent her a note: "I understand if you want me out of your life. I'll stay away, if that's what you want," but I never heard back. I sent her notes and emails with no response. I sent her birthday cards, called and left messages. Gradually, my pride kept me from reaching out to Brahna anymore and soon we didn't talk or communicate at all. I spent a lot of nights killing myself, brooding over a stiff drink, thinking about how I blew the one relationship that should have meant more than all the rest.

CHAPTER NINETEEN

Abandoned and broke

I was chasing that elusive butterfly. I was on that constant search for happiness and approval, alienating the people that never cared how far I could throw a football or how fast I could drive a car. I thought about what Brahna said when she said she wouldn't know me if we passed on the street. It made me think of my mother. I always wanted mom to experience the perfect family, so after football and with my racing career on hold, I went on a binge trading in wives and families, trying to find happiness. It was my latest competition–find the perfect picture of a family. When mom gave me that one-dollar bill that I'd signed as a kid and put in dad's coat pocket at his funeral, she may have been trying to tell me not to lose sight of Brahna. No matter how much money and fame I had, or how much I struggled with money and relationships, Brahna needed her dad.

I never got the chance to ask mom if that's what she really was trying to tell me. Mom was diagnosed with Alzheimer's Disease and it advanced pretty quickly. I took it hard. I visited mom at the home where my sister Annette admitted her and took mom out to dinner. When I picked her up, I was encouraged. She gave me a big kiss, called me by my name and said she was so happy to see me. Not 10-minutes later as we drove to dinner, mom turned to me and asked, "Where are we going and who are you?"

"I'm your son, mom, I'm your youngest, Dante. We're going to dinner."

She looked uncomfortable, confused and nervous the entire time we were at the restaurant. She began to tremble and looked terrified, so I made sure she ate something and took her right home. As I helped her out of the car, mom looked me in the eyes and said, "Hi, honey! When did you get here?"

It crushed me. Mom was the most fun person I ever knew and always wanted the family to be together and close. We just never fulfilled that dream of hers. But I kept trying.

Dena and I were miserable together in Vail. We rarely were together and both knew our marriage wouldn't last. I got invited to an NFL Alumni golf tournament in Houston, so of course I went. I knew Windi Akins from various other events I previously did in Houston and Windi was at the NFL Alumni tournament. Windi was a knockout and an attorney from Houston. I actually met her at a softball game that I played several years earlier. At the softball field, I saw a hot blonde with big boobs drive up in a Porsche and I thought, "Hmm, my kind of girl." I spoke with her on and off for years, but at the NFL tournament, Windi and I spent several days and nights together. We fell for each other quickly and just like that decided we were perfect for each other. I called Dena in Vail and told her, "I'm not coming back."

But as quickly as we fell for each other, we fell apart. My relationship with Windi was turbulent, never should have happened and was doomed from the start. We got a divorce after one crazy year.

That's how sick and desperate I was for some kind of direction and stability. I had no job, no money. I had nothing and I didn't have much to sell. I thought if I married Windi things would get better between us, but they never did. Before I left her, fifteen years after I sued Al Davis, I finally beat him and he was ordered to pay me. But by the time he did, all the money was gone because of back-taxes, divorce and bankruptcy. Al Davis turned my life into a game of vengeance and wanted to ruin me. He just about did. Whenever someone asked me about Al Davis I usually said, "I wouldn't piss in his mouth if his lungs were on fire." And I wouldn't. He's a scumbag.

Al held up paying on my contract so long, all the court battles and money problems that I had because of it ate up every dollar. I spent a lot of days and nights asking myself why I made so many bad decisions. Did people screw me over? Or did I let myself get screwed over?

I wasn't dumb, just a trusting person and probably too trusting. It constantly bit me. I was like my father, living in a Utopian world, where if I gave you my word, I wouldn't screw you over. But that wasn't the real world. My sister Annette took advantage, too, when mom finally died in '98. Butch was executor of dad's Will and dad had stipulated that I get a larger portion of their assets, because of all the money I had given him over the years. Butch understood. But when mom got sick, Annette became executor of the Will and after she put mom in the home, had Power Of Attorney and changed the Will, stipulating that the four kids get only equal shares. Butch knew the truth and I knew the truth, but after mom died, I didn't even fight it. I had so many other legal and money troubles I just thought, "OK, Annette, I guess that's what I mean to you."

Mom died in her sleep. She took a nap one day and never woke up. At her funeral, I saw Dorothy and Stan and mostly ignored them. I knew Stan remembered my talk with him in 1972, my promise that when mom and dad were gone, "I'll have your ass."

I had no intention of hurting Stan, but at mom's funeral I couldn't help but walk up behind him and tell Stan, "Don't forget what I said." And I walked away.

My sisters and I never were close and after what Dorothy and Stan did, after what Annette did, it guaranteed we never would be. Butch and I always stayed close. His son, my nephew, Todd, came to visit me in Houston while I searched for a job. I still dreamed about getting a racing team together, but Todd told me about a product he was developing called with DataWorks Plus, a digital photographic management system for law enforcement agencies. It eliminated a lot of paper work and could be used in court and in investigations. Todd was like my little brother and everything I hoped to turn out to be—a great father and a great guy. When he asked me if I wanted a job with his company, DataWorks Plus, I took it because I looked forward to working with him. I loved him. I needed work and working with people, marketing and selling myself and a product, was something I enjoyed.

I began calling on law enforcement agencies, selling the DataWorks technology for crime scene and mug shot management. Dan Pastorini working with law enforcement? It was a punch-line for all my friends, but I actually wound up getting agencies in Kansas, Oklahoma, Nebraska, Louisiana and Texas to use the enhance-able photos and data. It was just another competition.

I never let go of trying to get a race team together, running my own business and living the lifestyle I enjoyed, but I was escaping.

I didn't enjoy dealing with the police and sheriff's departments, but I worked my own hours and it was a living. I wanted to get away–sort of regroup, huddle. I moved to the country, northwest of Houston, outside a small town called Chappell Hill. It was a long commute for work and the events and appearances I did in Houston, but I wanted it that way. I became a bit of a recluse. I had a secluded place in the country, my escape in the woods. I guess with mom and dad gone now, I was going back to my roots, living on a little piece of land that had all sorts of wildlife and woods. I kept chasing that elusive butterfly. It was a character flaw I knew I had, but I couldn't explain it or kick it. Every opportunity that people put in front of me looked attractive and made sense, until something went awry. Every woman I fell for always seemed perfect, loving me for who I was. But when we got serious or married, they tried to change me and things fell apart.

I met Karen Zuntych at a bar in Houston one night when I went out with my attorney. She was a single mom. When we first started going out, I felt sorry for her. She had a hard time raising her son alone and I wanted to rescue her. We started dating, she moved in with me at the house in Chappell Hill and we got married in 2000.

There was that picture again. I had a house in the country, a tractor, dogs. Her kid wanted a pig, we got a pig. He wanted chickens, we got chickens. I taught her kid how to hunt and took him with me just about everywhere. I bought him his first truck. I was away from everybody and except for my appearance and job obligations, I was just trying to disappear. We had a great house in Washington County. By 2003, I was climbing the walls trying to get back into racing, hoping to build a racing team that could run road courses. It was a slow process selling DataWorks to law agencies, having to go through so much red tape, so I had time to build a plan for another team.

The first thing I had to do was lose some weight. Between living fat on the farm, literally, and drinking and eating at so many golf and charity events, I found myself about 40-pounds overweight. I had to fit into a car before I could drive one. Just like living in the country, drinking was my escape. I always drank. It was part of my life. My entire life, everything I did was a drinking environment. When I went out with my teammates or partied with friends, we had binge drinking. I drank to relax. I drank to celebrate. It was part of my daily routine, just like over-eating. When I was bored or felt trapped, which was happening at my place in Washington County by 2003, I looked for something to drink. When Karen and I argued, I would go drink. I had a lot of pain in my life and not a lot of true love, so I drank to make it better.

In 2003, I was playing golf with Jay Mincks, a great guy and executive vice-president of sales and marketing for Insperity, a provider of HR and business performance solutions. I had a great relationship with Insperity, doing several charity events with them. I loved the way they operated. They got things done. Jay asked how I was doing and I told him, "You know, I'm just not happy."

We talked for a while about my ambition to eventually put a team together and enter the Grand Am or American Le Mans Sports Car Series. The only thing that truly made me happy, the only thing I tirelessly worked at and always was in my soul was racing. My house was not far from Texas World Speedway, so I went up there and drove cars occasionally and kept in contact with all my racing friends. I wanted to do road racing. I wanted to get Pastorini Racing going again. I eventually could put a team together and have several cars in Grand Am racing.. I had the knowledge and ambition to do it. I just didn't have the sponsor.

Jay asked me to put a budget together and we'd talk about it. I put a marketing package together, met with Jay, gave him a price on how much it would cost to put a racing team together and a deal was made.

I partnered with Sam Shalala again, Juergen Steiner became the crew chief and we built the Porsche we would race. It was the nicest Porsche we ever built. There was a lot of attention to detail and it raced great. For more than a year, we developed our team, tested the car, ran the car in events to get me experience and everyone loved the partnership.

When the sponsorship with Insperity ended, I made calls everywhere trying to find another sponsor and came up empty, but my friend Betty Johnston loved racing and knew the potential my team had. I knew Betty for 12 years, teaming with her on so many charity events over the years. She was a very successful businesswoman, was deeply involved in NFL Charities and after asking me what it would take to get back into racing, established DP7 Racing. She was committed.

We tried to buy a Mercedes that we could race, which would put Mercedes back on the road circuit, which they hadn't done in years. That deal fell through, when a partner in Florida, Hartmut Fehyl, breached our contract and did not build the car in time. The car never got off the ground. He basically took the money we sent to start on the project, $160,000, and ran. When we severed that relationship because the car wasn't getting built, he filed suit on us, saying we owed him money. We won the suit in Florida and were awarded $750,000, but he decided to file bankruptcy. We wound up settling for pennies on the dollar—$160,000. It was a mess, because at the same time Lamborghini approached us and we built another car with the same group of people. It was a huge mistake. It was a dog car. We took the Lamborghini to the Specialty Equipment Market Association show, the largest car show in the world, with about 100,000 people in the business attending. We were looking for potential sponsorships and partners, and the car got more notoriety than any other car at the SEMA show. It looked fantastic, but was a bad car. We spent way too much trying to get it to run fast. It became an embarrassment for me, listening to the wrong people, and costing Betty a lot of money. The crooks in racing saw someone like Betty come along and took advantage of her. She could have been great for racing. Everywhere we went, we touted Betty as the First Lady of motorsports, but it was an opportunity that failed. I hated that it hurt Betty. She finally had enough, got out of racing and I understood. We shut the doors and that was it. We built the car for more than $1 million and wound up selling it for $160,000. It looked fantastic, but was a shit box of a race car.

Karen and I had long been having troubles and we wound up divorcing after she accused me of an affair, which for once I wasn't having. Then Karen accused me of domestic violence, which was another lie. We had an argument and she called the police. When the officers arrived, they realized I hadn't done anything and Karen was just trying to get me out of the house. It worked. After our divorce, I decided to get out of Chappell Hill, it was such a small town and everybody was talking about our divorce. I sold the house and property, but didn't keep any of the profits. What I didn't settle with Karen, the I.R.S. took.

I moved back into Houston, into a house Betty owned where she let me stay rent-free until I could get back on my feet. I made a vow to myself. Five marriages were enough. I retired from marriage. That's one sport I just wasn't very good at.

CHAPTER TWENTY

Face-down on the floor of the bar

When I was a kid, I was like everyone else. I thought when you became a successful pro athlete your life was set. When Betty let me live at the house she owned, I couldn't have been more humbled, but also thankful for my real friends who always helped and always were there. I actually felt fortunate after my divorce from Karen, because I knew I had great friends and so many contacts over the years that I could call on and trust. I learned the hardest thing to do was ask for a job and the other hardest thing to do was sign autographs in an unemployment line. But I did them. I refused to quit, so I wasn't going to quit now.

How many times did I get knocked on my ass? But I took pride in picking myself up and getting ready for the next play, believing the next one would be the one. It was just like football. I got knocked on my ass in business, so I huddled up with my closest friends and kept looking for the next opportunity. When an engine blew on the race track, I pulled out the tool chest and worked with the team to fix it and get back on the road. When a relationship went sour, I moved on. I never conceded defeat on anything, until my divorce with Karen when I realized I just was not cut out to be married. In my mind, I wadded up that perfect picture of the perfect family I always envisioned and tossed it away.

Everything became easier for me. I loved doing client relations and business development events with Insperity. I did similar work for Texpo, an energy company. I did speaking engagements on life lessons, the realities of an NFL life and leadership. As always, I helped golf and charity events, because even when I was at my lowest I considered it my responsibility.

My publicist and friend Karen Henry invited me to a Ralph Lauren Christmas party that was hosted by former Oilers tackle Ray Childress and his wife Kara. I was mingling and sharing stories with folks, when I saw a remarkably beautiful woman walking straight across the room toward me. She asked if she could take a picture with me and then said, "I'm a big fan."

I looked at her and said, "You're not old enough to remember me."

"You'd be surprised."

Her name was Pam and we wound up talking all night. It turned out she was four-years older than me, but just incredible. What can I say? I've always loved older women. Later, when I found out she moved out and was divorcing her husband, I began talking with her more. It was amazing I never had met Pam before. When I went out with her, as many people knew her as knew me. She was a school teacher that had worked for Ralph Lauren for years and always was around the same people I was around. She knew my friend Barry Warner when and Barry and I ran around together. She dated the attorney that represented me against Beverly, Ron Ramey. How the hell we never met or knew each other before was beyond me.

I guessed the time wasn't right back then, because I never would have realized what I had with Pam. I told myself constantly that I didn't want to get serious with Pam, but I found myself constantly gravitating back to her. I realized for the first time that everybody has shortcomings in life and I didn't have to try and be perfect, or be something for the sake of other people. Pam made me feel like I could let things happen instead of trying to make things happen. They say you never know when you're going to find true love, but you'll know it when you do. I found it with Pam, without ever even looking.

Pam was beautiful on the inside, not jealous or hurt by anything I'd done in my past and life was easy with her. We never had a cross word and I loved everything about her family. It turned out Pam knew me growing up in Baytown, but really wasn't a big football fan. She told me the story of her sister Cathy being head over heels in love with Luv Ya Blue. Whenever Pam called Cathy on a Sunday and asked, "What are you doing?" Cathy answered, "It's Sunday afternoon. What do you think I'm doing? I'm watching Dan Pastorini!"

Pam's mother, who everyone called Meemaw, was in her late-'90s and was a joy. Her birthday was the exact same day as my mother's.

Pam also convinced me to swallow my pride and pain and reconnect with Brahna. I was embarrassed about how I wasn't there for Brahna and just put up a wall between us.

"That's your daughter," Pam told me early in 2009. "You need to call her. You need to bug her until she gets tired of it and calls you back just to shut you up."

I called for weeks. I emailed and texted. I just kept calling and leaving messages for Brahna, finally leaving a message as I was headed to Long Beach for a race, "Look, Brahna, I'm racing in Long Beach. I miss you. I'd love to have some friendly faces in the stands."

She finally answered me and came to the race. I told her how much I missed her and loved her. I told her I realized I never was a poster dad by any means, and maybe I never would be. I told her I knew I was a jackass. But we communicated more often and talked more often, until it was almost as if there never was a problem between us. I traveled to Long Beach whenever I could to see her. Whenever we talked, I told her I loved her and she told me she loved me.

I couldn't thank Pam enough for helping me bring my daughter back into my life. Pam agreed with my retirement from marriage plan–she didn't want to get married, either. But I did ask her about moving in together. She was reluctant, because she didn't know how her kids would react.

Pam called Meemaw on her 96th birthday and said, "Dan asked me to move in with him."

"What'd you tell him?"

"I told him I didn't think we should."

That's when Meemaw showed a little fire that would make any Pastorini proud.

"You have ruined my day," Meemaw told Pam. "You have ruined my birthday. If you don't move in with that man you are out of your mind. And don't bother coming home, because I'll go with him."

Five-minutes later Pam called me and said, "I guess we're moving in together."

When I was with Pam, I drank less than I ever had. If we went to dinner or an event, I would have one glass of wine, that's about it. But in April of '10, I was invited to a weekend charity golf event for the Boys and Girls Clubs in Bryan-College Station and Pam couldn't go. I went to a cocktail reception, dinner and fundraiser on Sunday night and had about six beers and some tequila shots. I wasn't drunk when I left. The event lasted about six-hours. There had been many a night when six beers and tequila shots were packed into an hour. As I drove back to my hotel, I passed a bar, saw that it had pool tables and thought, "I'm gonna shoot some pool and get one more for the road."

I drove up to the bar in my Mercedes and walked into the place dressed pretty nicely, with Ralph Lauren slacks and a nice shirt. I looked like I was rich. I ordered a beer—one beer. And then everything became hazy.

I was used to going into places and feeling people looking at me, but this was different. It just felt different. The next thing I knew, I was lying face-down on the floor of the bar, telling myself to get up. The more I tried to stand up, the more I kept falling down. I never experienced anything like it. I'd been drunk a lot in the past, but never like this. I couldn't straighten up. I said, "How did I fall down?"

It was as if I was in a fog, or in a dream. I started getting pushed and grabbed. I got to the door and someone shoved me to the ground. Then, someone started hitting me several times. Someone kicked me in the ass with a boot and knocked me down again and I thought, "I've got to get to my car."

Ever since '72, the first time my car was vandalized, I always carried some kind of protection with me. I had a Taser gun in my car, so I began crawling and stumbling toward my car. The same two faces that watched me in the bar kept following me. When I got to my car, thank God I had keyless entry. I hit the button, the door opened, I grabbed my Taser and turned to the two guys.

"Back off!"

One guy lunged at me and–boom–I Tasered him and he locked up. His buddy came at me and I hit him with the wand. That's the last thing I remembered.

I woke up in the back of a Bryan emergency medical vehicle. I had a bruise on my arm, a boot-mark on the back of my pants and scrapes everywhere on my arms. Somehow, I got in my car and sped off, hitting a car at a stoplight, spinning him and pushing his car into an oncoming car. Nobody got hurt, thank God.

At the hospital, when they took my blood I asked if they could check for other drugs. I was coherent enough to ask about that, but they didn't. I was taken to Brazos County jail, booked and checked into jail at 3 a.m. I later was told I had an extremely high blood-alcohol level. I was not allowed to leave jail until after my blood-alcohol level was below .08. At 7:30 a.m. they checked my blood-alcohol level and it already had come down to a .082. I was confused. How the heck did my blood-alcohol level go down so fast? And if my blood-alcohol level at the hospital was so high, why was I talking coherently on the police video? The only two people who could prove I might have been drugged by a couple of guys trying to rob me were those two guys and they weren't coming forward. All I could prove for certain was that I was stupid. If I hadn't been drinking, I wouldn't have put myself in that position. If I hadn't wanted one more for the road, I would never have had my face on the floor of that bar. It was my fault.

As I sat in jail, I was a mess. I thought to myself, "Why are you trying to blame something or someone else? You did this to yourself. You've done this to yourself over and over again. You've always done this to yourself."

When I was released, I was well enough to still play in the Boys and Girls Club golf tournament. When I got home that night and saw Pam, she told me, "The only thing that could ever come between us is your drinking."

That's all I needed to hear. I realized right there that I needed Pam in my life a lot more than I needed drinking. Pammy is my angel. I looked her in the eyes.

"I promise you, Pam, I never will drink again. I mean it. Never."

She told me we didn't have to decide anything right then and maybe I could just cut down, but I told her again, "I mean it. I'm done."

Bum called my cell phone less than half an hour later.

"How ya doin?" he told me. Then he paused and said, "You know . . ."

I stopped him before he could say anything else.

"I know what you're going to say, Bum. Save it. I've promised Pam. I'll promise you, too, coach. I'm done. I'll never drink again. You'll never see anything like what happened associated with me again."

Bum told me, "Well, we've been down this road before. I know you're a man of your word. If you say you're done, you're done. That's good enough for me. I love you and I'm here for you no matter what."

CHAPTER TWENTY-ONE

"It's a breathalyzer"

I didn't know if I was an alcoholic or not. I never craved alcohol and never sneaked a drink or drank somewhere where I shouldn't have been drinking. I never drank while I worked. But I knew I definitely was a problem drinker. If I had one drink, I had to have two and then more. I used alcohol as a badge of honor and a sign of camaraderie. It was just part of the culture. I smoked, drank, dipped tobacco. Had the accident not happened, I wouldn't be where I was with Pam and building a good business.

When I went to my court date in Brazos County, I realized the best thing for me to do was get the incident behind me and move on. The judge was a very reasonable lady. I was compliant with everything she asked of me before the hearing, so the prosecutor offered two years' probation, community service and a number of other fines and classes. I didn't hide from my mistake and everything in my life that led to that moment in Bryan. I had to pay the price just like everybody else and I knew it. I didn't fight it. No matter what I thought happened, there was no justification for what I did. There were no witnesses. The smoking gun was my blood test.

I lost my license as result of what I did. I had to get a special license and identification card that I had to carry throughout my probation. It identified me as a convicted criminal. I could only drive to and from work and community service events. I had to get a portable breath analyzer. Every time I traveled for business or a charity event, I had to notify my probation office and ask for a travel permit. When I left town and when I returned, I had to go to the probation office for a urinalysis.

A few months into my probation, as I complied with everything and never had a drop of alcohol, I partnered with my long-time drag-racing friend, Lee Donabedian on a spice and rub called, "Dan Pastorini's Texas-style Rub." Lee, like me, had a long family history in the restaurant industry. For years anytime we were together, usually at the Christmas for Children event Lee had at his Rube's Restaurant, we would start cooking and throwing together spices in the kitchen. We always talked about marketing our favorite spices. Lee finally said, "Let's do this rub thing" and the rub has taken off. We debuted it at the Houston Livestock Show & Rodeo, the biggest barbecue cook-off in the world, and it was a hit. But marketing and getting it into stores required a lot of travel on my part and a different kind of scrambling, trying to stay compliant with my probation.

Between 7 a.m. and 10 a.m. and 7 p.m. and 10 p.m. every day I had to blow on my portable breathalyzer machine. As I blew on the machine, it took a picture of me doing it. Every day, twice a day, for an entire year I had to test myself and it registered the result with my probation office. When I drove to stores or meetings, I had an adapter for the machine in my car, so I could take the test. When I went to Las Vegas for a meeting, as I put my bags through security, a TSA agent held up the machine and announced in front of everyone in line, "What's this?"

I just shook my head.

"It's a breathalyzer."

The flight left Houston at 6:55 p.m. I thought I could take the breath test on the plane, but there was not a power outlet on the plane. When we landed at 8:15 Las Vegas time–10:15 Houston time—I rushed to a docking station on the airport concourse and sat there blowing into a breathalyzer, as people walked back and forth. That's the only time I was late taking the test, by only 15-minutes, but I tested clean and my probation officer was good with it.

I told her, "I don't drink. I don't take drugs. I'm breathing into this thing twice a day. When I come in here, I blow for you again. I'm not sneaking any booze. I'm not doing anything. I've gone through a lot of embarrassing stuff and I know it's my fault. But everyone knows who I am. I'm signing autographs with a breathalyzer machine in one hand."

The probation office was sympathetic and became more flexible with meetings, although I still fulfilled every detail of the terms of my probation. I went through a victims' class at the courthouse. I did 80-hours of community service. The court allowed me to use some of the charity work I always did as community service, so long as I got documentation from the director of each charity. That was embarrassing, asking for To Whom It May Concern letters that I could take to my probation officer. It was a series of embarrassing things, but I did it. I paid the fines, the court costs and went to three four-hour DWI classes. I had an alcohol evaluation. When I went in to pee in a cup, one of the guys working there said, "Hey, Mr. Pastorini, I loved you with the Oilers. Can you sign this?"

I went to Alcoholics Anonymous meetings.

I was called upon. I stood up and said, "Hi, I'm Dan, and I'm an alcoholic."

I told my story. I told everyone I met, no matter how embarrassing the situation, "I did the crime. I'm trying to do my time."

It didn't take long for me to see everything so much clearer when I stopped drinking. I felt better and everybody started coming up to me, telling me how good I looked. I dedicated myself to not drinking anymore. It was a personal challenge, but it never was as tough for me to quit as I thought it would be, because I had that reward. I had Pam. I had my great relationships with Insperity and Texpo and working on my spice rub with a couple of friends I've known for 25-years—guys that I knew I could trust—was comforting and reassuring.

The last time I sat in the probation office waiting room, I was relieved it finally was over. I also had the same feeling I had the first time I sat in that probation office. It was the same feeling I had standing in an unemployment line.

I asked myself, "How did you get to this point?"

It was demeaning and embarrassing. I sat with some pretty rough people in that waiting room, but I deserved to be there. I felt everyone's eyes on me, like I always did. I signed some autographs. I sat there telling myself, "A smart person learns from this and you're a smart person."

I thought, "I'm never going to hide from this. Every person I come across, I want them to know what I've gone through. I want them to know stardom or money doesn't change the fact that it's not a matter of if, but when. If you drink and drive you're going to get caught and you're going to hurt people."

I told myself, "This never will happen to you again. You never again will be in this place."

And I never will.

EPILOGUE

There were a lot of low points in my life. I lost all self-confidence and was a beaten man. I lost every dollar, every marriage, anesthetized myself with booze and was a nasty drunk. I sat in a jail cell and was a bad father.

I was a tough guy who was a fragile man. The lifestyle I had once meant everything to me. I took pride in being the guy with a swagger. I enjoyed it. There was nothing more important than being what I was, where I was, living the life I did. I had experiences and moments some people wouldn't have in ten lifetimes and, man, what a ride it was.

What we had in Houston never again will be duplicated, because there never again will be a city so uninhibited and untamed, exploding with growth, money and optimism. We were what Houston was. Houston was a roughneck town and we were a roughneck team. Like Bum always said, we weren't pretty dancers but we danced every dance. My racing career–whether on dirt, water, drag strips, ovals or road courses—was an unpredictable, unbelievable adventure. My off-field antics and conquests, for better and worse, were like scenes from a movie. It was all so fairytale and surreal.

And when the last dollar finally was sucked away and my dignity was stripped bare, when nobody gave a damn anymore, I realized I never was owed a damn thing. The only thing I want now is what I always wanted—a fair opportunity to compete and a fair chance to work, just like anybody else in this world.

I have regrets, but no excuses. The good Lord gave me gifts and dealt me a hand. I played it to the fullest. I'm willing to see what He's got next for me. I'm not the richest man in the world, but I can live with myself. I never screwed anyone over and I never will. I'm alright. I have the greatest woman in my life, great friends, great support and I'm in business with dear friends who are like brothers to me.

Becoming sober was a revelation. I understand now that there are so many things we all have going for us. You don't realize it until you scrape the bottom; until your face is on the floor of a bar or wherever it is you crash.

I always searched for that elusive answer for total happiness. I had it brow-beaten in my head that I had to be married in order to be happy. For me, that was the furthest thing from the truth. It only affected my ability to have a successful marriage and be faithful to my wives. I don't really know why I did the things I did when it came to women. Some of the relationships were infatuations. Some were because I thought that's how it was supposed to be.

Now, I have the closest thing to the perfect family I've ever had and it's imperfect. That's what makes it great. It's heartwarming to realize I can celebrate Christmas with Meemaw, Pam's ex-husband, Pam's kids, my daughter and it's still perfect. There is a lot of love in Pam's family and they've made me a part of it. I've got friends that are family, too. Carl is an intimidating, irritating guy with a filthy mouth and a heart of gold. He's my brother. Bum is in his late-'80s with bad hearing. He is like my father. I ran hard for a lot of years, but now I have direction. I can't put my finger on exactly what it is, but there's a comfort that I feel every morning when I wake up.

Looking through the fence near the corner of Fannin and Braeswood, I realized something. Schmitty was right all along. I finally got the world by the tail.

ABOUT JOHN P. LOPEZ

John is a regular contributor for SportsIllustrated.com and TexAgs.com, as well as co-host of CBS Houston's morning sports talk show, Vandermeer & Lopez. John also has written for the Bryan Eagle, San Antonio Express-News and the Houston Chronicle.

He has been named Texas' best sports columnist and earned national recognition from the Associated Press Managing Editors and Associated Press Sports Editors. He has appeared on The Today Show, ESPN Sports Center, Dateline NBC, CNN Sports at Night, CBS This Morning and ESPN's Outside The Lines. He has been a Baseball Hall of Fame voter since 1999 and a Heisman Trophy voter since 1985.

In 1997, John co-authored Landing On My Feet–A Diary Of Dreams, with 1996 Olympic gold medalist Kerri Strug. He has three children–Jacob, BG and Leah–and lives in Humble, Tx., with his wife, Jan, and loyal dog, Gibson.

Lightning Source UK Ltd.
Milton Keynes UK
UKOW051926231211

184356UK00001B/2/P